An African Feminist Philosophy of Language

This book calls for the institution of an African feminist philosophy of language, challenging existing debates and encouraging a move away from the Western gaze.

The book begins with an analysis of the philosophical context of African feminism and a call for the decolonization of epistemological discourse. Oyeleye then goes on to consider how indigenous patriarchies play out in the cultural reality of the Yorùbá in particular, ontologically unpacking the nature of woman as expressed in language, especially in myths and proverbs. Challenging the derogatory language found in proverbs which entrench patriarchal oppression, the author advocates for feminist postproverbials: new proverbs which draw on old traditions but reconstruct the space of woman in a new, egalitarian rhetorical tradition. The author concludes by outlining the conditions necessary for African feminist philosophers to consider language as a decolonizing space which can help to push through the agenda of social change.

This book will be an important resource for researchers from across the fields of gender and women studies, feminist philosophy, philosophy of language, cultural studies and African studies.

Olayinka Oyeleye holds a doctorate in philosophy from the University of Ibadan, Nigeria. Her research profile articulates an interdisciplinary platform that straddles African feminist philosophy, the philosophy of language and African gender and ethical discourses. Her essays have appeared in many distinguished publications.

Global Africa
Series Editors: Toyin Falola and Roy Doron

17. **Governance and Leadership Institutions in Nigeria**
    Edited by Ernest Toochie Aniche and Toyin Falola

18. **African Indigenous Knowledges in a Postcolonial World**
    Essays in Honour of Toyin Falola
    Edited by Olajumoke Yacob-Haliso, Ngozi Nwogwugwu and Gift Ntiwunka

19. **Nigerian Female Dramatists**
    Expression, Resistance, Agency
    Edited by Bosede Funke Afolayan

20. **Bessie Head and the Trauma of Exile**
    Identity and Alienation in Southern African Fiction
    Joshua Agbo

21. **Africa's Soft Power**
    Philosophies, Political Values, Foreign Policies and Cultural Exports
    Oluwaseun Tella

22. **The Life and Times of Chinua Achebe**
    Kalu Ogbaa

23. **Illicit Financial Flows from South Africa**
    Decolonial Perspectives on Political Economy and Corruption
    Edited by Serges Djoyou Kamga

24. **Sabelo Ndlovu-Gatsheni and African Decolonial Studies**
    Toyin Falola

25. **An African Feminist Philosophy of Language**
    Olayinka Oyeleye

For more information about this series, please visit: https://www.routledge.com

An African Feminist Philosophy of Language

Olayinka Oyeleye

LONDON AND NEW YORK

First published 2025
by Routledge
4 Park Square, Milton Park, Abingdon, Oxon OX14 4RN

and by Routledge
605 Third Avenue, New York, NY 10158

Routledge is an imprint of the Taylor & Francis Group, an informa business

© 2025 Olayinka Oyeleye

The right of Olayinka Oyeleye to be identified as author of this work has been asserted in accordance with sections 77 and 78 of the Copyright, Designs and Patents Act 1988.

All rights reserved. No part of this book may be reprinted or reproduced or utilised in any form or by any electronic, mechanical, or other means, now known or hereafter invented, including photocopying and recording, or in any information storage or retrieval system, without permission in writing from the publishers.

Trademark notice: Product or corporate names may be trademarks or registered trademarks, and are used only for identification and explanation without intent to infringe.

British Library Cataloguing-in-Publication Data
A catalogue record for this book is available from the British Library

Library of Congress Cataloging-in-Publication Data
Names: Oyeleye, Olayinka, author.
Title: An African feminist philosophy of language / Olayinka Oyeleye.
Description: New York : Routledge, 2024. | Series: [Global Africa] | Includes bibliographical references and index.
Identifiers: LCCN 2024026220 (print) | LCCN 2024026221 (ebook) | ISBN 9781032706320 (hardback) | ISBN 9781032706368 (paperback) | ISBN 9781032706382 (ebook)
Subjects: LCSH: Language and languages—Philosophy. | Sexism in language—Africa. | Feminist theory—Africa.
Classification: LCC P120.S48 O945 2024 (print) | LCC P120.S48 (ebook) | DDC 408.2096—dc23/eng/20240612
LC record available at https://lccn.loc.gov/2024026220
LC ebook record available at https://lccn.loc.gov/2024026221

ISBN: 978-1-032-70632-0 (hbk)
ISBN: 978-1-032-70636-8 (pbk)
ISBN: 978-1-032-70638-2 (ebk)

DOI: 10.4324/9781032706382

Typeset in Times New Roman
by Apex CoVantage, LLC

To the future of feminisms and to feminists yet unborn

Contents

Foreword		*viii*
Acknowledgements		*x*
	Introduction: On a Subversive Feminist Rhetoric	1
1	What Is Woman? Conceptualizing Feminisms	8
2	Feminist Scholarship and the Politics of Language in Africa	28
3	The Dehumanized Woman in History, Philosophy and Culture	43
4	Between Proverbs and Postproverbials	72
5	Towards an African Feminist Philosophy of Language	100
	Index	*114*

Foreword

It is a great pleasure and my good fortune to be able to welcome this brilliant offshoot of the postproverbial imagination. Postproverbiality, as a definable handle of transgressive paremiology, enables a deconstructive—or to trope on the Heideggerian root, a *destructuring*—force that undermines the structural layers of conventional or traditional thought and culture. The postproverbial deconstitutes the traditional proverbs in ways that initiate what Oyeleye and I regard as the "postproverbial agency" (2019). And that agency further enables a recuperation of voices, texts and meanings that had hitherto been submerged under the structural tyranny of traditional wisdom around which specific African cultures order meaning and existence.

The postproverbial imagination has long been embedded in the unconscious, modernist reaction to conventional African vernacular practice, and the veritable evidence of this is represented by Oyeleye's commendable and critical efforts to ground the agency it affords within the feminist's onslaught against proverbial oppression. While traditional African proverbs encode the wisdom of the ages, such "wisdom" is often gained at the expense of silencing and denigrating what it means to be a woman. Sexist proverbs demean, devalue and derogate femininity as the epiphenomenon of masculinity within cultural contexts that exult the phallic order. Feminist proverbial, the core of this brilliant new study, therefore becomes evident immediately as a subversive paremiological intrusion whose essence is to destructure the phallic constitution of what it means to be human.

However, and more significantly, Oyeleye transcends the deconstructive mandate of postproverbiality through a reconstructive and reformative model that seeks to initiate a radical and new rhetorical tradition within which the idea of a woman is properly rehumanized. The idea of rehumanization, to adapt Afolayan's (2023) mandate for a critical African philosophy, fits smugly within the feminist postproverbial since that mandate, according to him, serves as an emancipatory project that energizes the "autonomous African subject." In this case, the dehumanized subject is the African woman whose rehumanization requires a postproverbial *redescription* that "speaks to the Fanonian new humanism and the concepts and metaphilosophical frameworks by which we address the task" (Afolayan, 2023: 234). The task of rehumanization meets the postmodern orientation of postproverbiality halfway in reconstructing the new from the old (Raji-Oyelade, 2022).

The task that Oyeleye sets for herself in this new book is an ambitious one: it is to jumpstart a larger discourse around the subject matter of an African feminist philosophy of language. This is crucial at a rhetorical level since language denotes and connotes a significant proportion of what constitutes values and meanings for humans. This task therefore constitutes both a challenge and a blueprint. It is a challenge to African philosophy as androcentric and hence inattentive discipline that has neglected too long its participation in the phallic order that silences women. And what other way to break that silence than through the institution of a subversive paremiology that carries the postmodern burden of undermining the grand narrative of convention and oppression as well as the deliberate feminist philosophical inquiry into how language serves the patriarchal strangulation of the feminine? Oyeleye also provides a blueprint that challenges African (feminist) philosophers to pay more than a regular attention to the role that proverbiality plays in the oppression of the feminine and how postproverbiality stands a chance as the unique source for rescuing the humanity/womanity of the African woman—and indeed in redeeming the complicity of African philosophy itself.

A final word on methodology. Oyeleye is a child of many worlds and multiple experiences; and they all played critical parts in the interdisciplinarity that this new and bold study represents. From philosophy and paremiology to cultural studies, Oyeleye weaves a tight and compact defense of feminist postproverbiality. But more than this, the feminist postproverbial gesture at the urgency of the need to commence an African feminist philosophy of language that transcends the default argumentation around the place of language and linguistic interventions in postcolonial African philosophy to a more critical and substantive rhetorical tradition that (re)humanizes the woman. This interdisciplinary matrix makes *An African Feminist Philosophy of Language* a tour de force that African philosophers, feminists and cultural theorists must contend with in the collective attempts at apprehending the importance and flourishing of more humane gender relations on the continent.

Aderemi Raji-Oyelade.

References

Afolayan, Adeshina. 2023. "On critical African philosophy: Mapping the boundaries of a good philosophical tradition," *Metaphilosophy*, 54: 223–237.
Raji-Oyelade, Aderemi. 2012. *Playful Blasphemies: Postproverbials as Archetypes of Modernity in Yoruba Culture*. Trier: Wissenschaftlicher Verlag.
Raji-Oyelade, Aderemi and Oyeleye, Olayinka. 2019. "Introduction: Postproverbial Agency: Textrs, Media and Mediation in African Cultures," *Matatu*, 51.2: 229–240.

Acknowledgements

This book encodes multiple indebtednesses which I cannot possibly pay. However, for every single contribution – from the most innocuous suggestion to the most profound engagements – I am very grateful.

To Professor Oyeronke Oyewumi, many thanks for your thoughts and the books. Dr Mshai Mwangola, you emailed me a major text for this work. Dr Awino Okech, Professor Philomina Okeke-Ihejirika, thank you for your contributions and reviews and the wonderful time at CODESRIA Gender Institute, Senegal. Professor Nemata Blyden, thank you for your engagements with this work. Professor Alicia Decker, the African Feminist Initiative platform provided an opportunity to connect with numerous feminists who have contributed to the success of this work one way or another. Professor Nnaemeka, you are deeply appreciated.

To the lecturers in the Department of Philosophy, University of Ibadan, thank you. To Professor Adeshina Afolayan: a million words could never effectively express all I would like to say. To Professor Aderemi Raji-Oyelade, I'm still standing on your giant shoulders.

Moyosore, Moyinoluwa and Momoyioluwa: this is all because of you. Thank you to my family and friends, for always and forever.

Introduction
On a Subversive Feminist Rhetoric

Language, a central feature of human communication and existence, is crucial to cultural survival and dynamics: it serves as a repository for cultural production and is essentially the linguistic carrier of a people's cultural and historical achievements. Language serves as the marker of the collective norms and values by which people identify themselves as belonging to the same culture, especially in opposition to other people who do not share these values and norms. Claire Kramsch (2003, 3) outlines three functions that language performs in relation to culture: "Language expresses a cultural reality," meaning that our attitudes, beliefs and worldviews find expression in language; "language embodies a cultural reality" in the sense that people create new experiences through language; and lastly, "language symbolises a cultural reality" in the sense that each sign and symbol are already value laden. Here lies the problem: a cultural reality represents the context for both wholesome and less-than-wholesome practices. Most African cultures are patriarchal and engender a patriarchal hierarchization of biological differences. It is in this sense that it becomes significant to investigate language use and how it relates to the discourse on gender, and this is what gives the African feminist philosopher her first condition for the possibility of an African feminist philosophy of language.

Feminism's core problem remains the idea of who a woman is, and that problem is made even more daunting because it is buried under layers of cultural contexts and discourses. An African feminist philosophy of language (henceforth, AFPL) is therefore primarily concerned with analyzing the concept and meaning of woman and how these are often deployed in the African sociocultural and linguistic imagination, as well as through oral, written and popular cultures. Given the fact that Africa is culturally and linguistically heterogenous, a discourse on the meaning of woman opens a new and expansive discursive space through which we can gain a better understanding of the concept's *denotation*, its literal meaning; its *connotation*, which accounts for its emotive and cultural association and its *referent*, what it represents in that sociocultural space and perhaps even much more. Understanding the meanings and discursive ramifications of the idea of woman in specific African

DOI: 10.4324/9781032706382-1

languages is a crucial step in the decolonization of African feminist scholarship and an even more critical second condition for the emergence and commencement of AFPL.

The collaboration between African feminist scholarship and AFPL constitutes, as I see it, a significant pragmatic turn in the ongoing attempt to rethink African feminisms and jumpstart a subversive reformation and reconstructive transformation of the rhetorical space constituted by the epistemic violence of patriarchal linguistic and sociocultural practices. African feminist theorizing has expectedly focused on the virulence of African traditional proverbs as the site of this epistemic violence, and this has led to an emerging discursive significance of feminist postproverbials and their capacity for paremiological transgression. African feminist postproverbials are the opening act of AFPL, and I am glad to initiate its first salvo in this study.

However, it is important to note that the foundation for the take-off of AFPL was laid by pervading tensions within feminist scholarship in Africa and the formidable discursive engagements of many African feminist theorists. In focus here are the works of Oyeronke Oyewumi, Ifi Amadiume, Wanjira Muthoni, Helen Yitah and Obioma Nnaemeka, among many others. Oyewumi's (1997, 2004, 2005, 2016) and Amadiume's (1987) works are significant because they shifted the discourse on African feminism away from substantive theorization to a linguistic methodology that engaged with the language within which the discourse on (African) feminism is narrated. It would seem for both of them that understanding the concept of gender opens up vistas – linguistic, philosophical and ideological – which has enabled the reorientation of the debates and charted new theoretical paths.

Nnaemeka (1994) takes up the significance of Mariama Ba's understanding of the "liberating force of language" as the thread that allows her to navigate the contributions of Ba, Buchi Emecheta and Flora Nwapa to the inscriptions of the agential vice of African women and their struggles in literary texts as a means of reshaping the social texts. On their part, Muthoni (1994) and Yitah (2006, 2009) employed the more pragmatic approach of rewriting aspects of our oral tradition. While Muthoni opted to reconstruct old narratives imbued with gendered and patriarchal undertones, Yitah documented the proverbial rebellion of Kasena women who through a 'joking ship' subverted misogynistic proverbs. Both Muthoni's and Yitah's works show the affinity between orality and social transformation.

Accordingly, AFPL aims to situate itself radically in the interiors of both the oral and written traditions perceived as sites where feminist subversive and disruptive strategies can be deployed. I suggest in Chapter 4 how parody as a poststructural and postmodern tool is useful to this discourse and in Chapter 5 how it can facilitate a textual re-inscription of woman. AFPL is also aimed at infiltrating popular culture amid other spaces where the everyday lived experience of the woman is encountered.

This study is an exercise in the poststructural subversion of the discursive and rhetorical linguistic practices that undermine the everyday lived experiences of women. The idea of theorizing from women's everyday experiences[1] is fundamental to feminist analysis since it lends credence to the notion of women as a marginalized group excluded from academic knowledge production. With knowledge itself being modelled from sociocultural and political contexts, the construction of knowledge becomes a collective effort owned by the entirety of a people.

How have women experienced language use in their everyday social lives? Being a postmodern, poststructural and postcolonial African feminist discourse, AFPL seeks to address and redress everyday sexist language experienced by postcolonial African women. According to Simidele Dosekun, everyday sexism, a term associated with routine language use and acts that translate into gender stereotypes, is under-researched due to the methodological challenges of generating data about experiences perceived as trivial and ephemeral. Detailing analysis from tweets of subjects which she dubs "the empowered Nigerian woman," Dosekun deploys intersectionality to argue that while the tweets might be representative of the voices of elite Nigerian women, stories of "'elite everyday sexism' are still stories of sexism" (2023, 1442). The phrase "everyday sexism" is a fundamental example of how patriarchal linguistic hegemonies dominate rhetorical spaces.

Rhetoric is the study and use of language. It examines how language is used in the construction of meanings and identities, in the coordination and maintenance of social groups, for social control and transformation and in the construction of knowledge. Rhetoric as employed in everyday communication and life uses persuasive language and "responds to disruptive events that reveal gaps in our habits, laws, beliefs and relationships by creating and publicizing a discourse that gives a new meaning to situations, audiences, beliefs and actions in order to promote certain possibilities over others" (Crick 2014, 254). Simply put, rhetoric has perpetually addressed the ways language shapes, reflects and changes practices among members of particular communities.

Rhetoric is also an artifact.[2] It is not natural to any given community but is made intentionally to accomplish some purpose and is often of cultural or historical interest. Rhetoric then as a cultural and historical artifact reflects the values of the society that creates it. The silencing of women, the invincibility of women, the othering of women, the misogynistic and sexist identities that have been assigned to women, all have been persuasively engrained through a patriarchal narrative, a play on power. Therefore, a necessary means of disempowering this patriarchal narrative is for feminists to find new rhetorical forms. To successfully change the status quo then, feminists, particularly African feminists, need to pay significant attention to language as a critical component of cultural expressivity, be well grounded in the knowledge of their culture, possess good control of the language of that culture and, through these, create alternative rhetorical forms.

Some pertinent questions arise that we might want to ask at this point: How did we get here? Why do we need a subversive feminist rhetoric? The issues, discourse and problematics of gender and the woman question have always been elucidated within the contexts of culture and history, especially with the intellectual ferment that greeted the emergence of African feminism as a rebellious offshoot of Western and Black feminisms. This dearth became more scandalous because of the significant absence of an engaging AFPL which could serve as the most critical point for engaging the linguistic structure of oppression within which gender liberation has been circumscribed.

Nkiru Nzegwu, a renowned feminist and African philosopher, argues that gender subordination in Africa can be traced to colonization and African men's views and constructions of the family (2006, 2). She contends that because this male-dominant view of the family has never been challenged, it has gained legitimacy and paramount importance. These arguments prompt the question, What informed the views of these African men regarding the family? Is it culture or colonization? What made these views a norm? What made the women accept it unchallenged? Nzegwu pays more attention to familial concerns than language because "the stability of a nation state depends on stable functioning families" (2006, 5). Another visible area of interest for Nzegwu is African arts and aesthetics.

Abosede Priscilla Ipadeola advances an approach founded on the principles of equality of the sexes irrespective of the intersections of race, class, status or gender. She suggests as well that issues that pertain to the discourse on women should be made prominent within the field of African philosophy (2023, xi). Blaming the androcentric nature of African philosophy on its 'maleness,' Ipadeola admonishes that beyond tackling Eurocentric ideologies, African philosophy should take an inward look into issues of women's oppression and also condemn the "cherished cultural elements, properties and practices that continue to bolster the marginalization of African women both on the continent and in the diaspora" (2023, xii). Laudable as this argument is, its concerns are also not linguistically oriented. In *Postethnophilosophy*, Sanya Osha dedicates a chapter to the figures of the African female with these aims for the chapter:

> (1) to trace the figure of woman within the specificity of African forms of discourse and to examine how she has been articulated and disarticulated and the ways through which she has reacted to these external mechanisms of power in both textual and existential terms; (2) to interrogate the contours of African feminist discourse in relation to patriarchal culture on the one hand, and forms of Western feminist theory on the other; (3) to give an indication of how terms such as sexuality, gender, and the body can be rethought in light of contemporary feminist theory and practice; and (4) to

indicate a new direction for African philosophy from the advances made by feminist discourse in general.

(2011, 115–116)

While Osha misses out on the significance of interrogating the linguistic underpinning of female oppression in Africa, and how language provides a crucial leeway to redressing patriarchal hegemonies, his call for a new direction for African philosophy marks this linguistic turn in African feministic scholarship and the emergence of AFPL as the discursive space for infiltrating, subverting and disrupting sexist, misogynistic and androcentric rhetorical traditions and linguistic hegemonies.

This book is divided into five chapters. Chapter 1 traces the trajectory of woman, exploring the controversial nature of the concept. Then I identify core concepts that demand critical (re)analysis within (African) feminist scholarship. I review critically canonical texts that underscore feminist theorizing in Africa and how, through theories and counter theories, gender has been misconstrued, feminism's core goals alienated and the condition of woman misrepresented.

In Chapter 2, I question if Western epistemological impositions have truly affected Africa's mode of knowledge production. I consider the implications of these impositions on the African mode of thinking, examining decolonization through the works of postcolonial and decolonial theorists like Said, Fanon, Gramsci, Spivak, Quijano and Mignolo. I delineate Wiredu's conceptual decolonization as a possible solution to a successful decolonization of thoughts and concepts, suggesting this method as a necessary first step for any African feminist discourse aimed at decolonizing oppressive discourses and practices. In decolonizing thinking, we must decolonize the language of thoughts. A section of this book is dedicated to a brief analysis of the philosophy of language, poststructuralism and the African philosophy of language as well. In the last section, I consider the academe both a colonial and a liberatory space.

Chapter 3 provides a critical interrogation of the sociology of patriarchy, exploring not just its supposed origins but its antithesis: matriarchy. I embark on a metaphysical interrogation of the Yorùbá idea of personhood, touching on the ontological question about the nature of woman as being or becoming. This ontological unpacking allows us to fathom the tripartite categorization around which a woman is endeared as a girl child, disparaged as a woman and valorized as 'mother'/older woman. This categorization makes possible fluid gender roles for females and a fixed one for males. The chapter's methodological leeway is in exploring some aspects of the Yorùbá oral history including the Ifá literary corpus as well as the Ìjálá poetic liturgy in order to better comprehend notions of gender and the power relations they engender and that are embedded in Yorùbá language use.

Chapter 4 considers the nature of proverbs as a necessary rather than contingent attribute of language. I particularly consider the epistemic significance of proverbs in the entrenchment of patriarchal oppression, excavating proverbial language from some African cultures which derogate women and promote inequalities. I employ the idea of postproverbials, which authenticate the presence of fresh proverbs minted from old ones, possessing new meanings and ideals. These new proverbs with new meanings and new values, when appropriated for feminist purposes, are meant to facilitate the reconstruction of the traditional space of woman in ways that place the woman within a new, egalitarian rhetorical tradition. Adapting these postproverbials to the fundamental task of recuperating the idea of woman is what generates the concept of feminist postproverbial as a methodological framework around which this work is primarily hinged.

Chapter 5 moves beyond the exercise of feminist reconstructions of demeaning proverbial language into outlining the preliminary conditions necessary for the emergence of a discursive space that allows African feminist philosophers and theorists at large to take language seriously as a fundamental decolonizing space that can not only further the intellectual responsibilities of African feminists and feminist philosophers but also help push the agenda of social change. The chapter sets in dialogue major philosophical trends on language with its African feminist counterpart drawing parallels and distinctions, charting new theoretical paths and considering future prospects for the discipline.

Notes

1 See Gqola, P.D. (2001). Ufanele uqavile: Blackwomen, feminisms and postcoloniality in Africa; *Agenda: Empowering Women for Gender Equity* Bakare-Yusuf, B. (2003). Beyond Determinism: The Phenomenology of African Female Existence. *Feminist Africa*, Vol. 2, pp. 8–24; Dosekun, S. (2019). African Feminisms. *The Palgrave Handbook of African Women's Studies*. Eds. O. Yacob-Haliso, and T. Falola. Palgrave Macmillan.
2 See Preston, B. (2022). Artifact. *The Stanford Encyclopedia of Philosophy*. Eds. Edward N. Zalta, and Uri Nodelman https://plato.stanford.edu/archives/win2022/entries/artifact/; Brummett, B. (2018). *Rhetoric in Popular Culture* (Fifth edition). Los Angeles & London: Sage Publications, Inc.

References

Amadiume, I. 1987. *Male Daughters, Female Husbands: Gender and Sex in an African Society*. London: Zed books.
Crick, N. 2014. *Rhetoric and Events. Philosophy & Rhetoric*. University Park, PA: Penn State University Press, 47(3).
Dosekun, S. 2023. The Problems and Intersectional Politics of "#BeingFemaleinNigeria". *Feminist Media Studies*, 23(4):1429–1445. https://doi.org/10.1080/14680777.2022.2030386

Ipadeola, Abosede, P. 2023. *Feminist African Philosophy: Women and the Politics of Difference*. New York: Routledge
Kramsch, C. 2003. *Language and Culture*. Oxford: Oxford University Press.
Muthoni, W. 1994. "The Literary Road to Empowerment." *The Road to Empowerment*. Ed. Wanjiku Kabira and Wanjira Muthoni. Nairobi: African Women's Development Communication Network. 54–70.
Nnaemeka, O. 1994. From Orality Writing: African Women Writers and the (Re)Inscription of Womanhood. *Research in African Literatures*, 25(4). Indiana: Indiana University Press. pp. 137–157. Stable URL: http://www.jstor.org/stable/3819872. Accessed online 14 November 2017.
Nzegwu, N. 2006. *Family Matters: Feminist Concepts in African Philosophy of Culture*. New York: State University of New York Press.
Osha, S. 2011. *Postethnophilosophy*. Amsterdam & New York: Rodopi.
Oyewumi, O. 1997. *The Invention of Women: Making an African Sense of Gender Western Discourses*. Minneapolis: University of Minnesota Press.
Oyewumi, O. 2004. Conceptualising Gender: The Eurocentric Foundations of Feminist Concepts and the Challenge of African Epistemologies. *African Gender Scholarship Concepts*. Dakar: Senegal.
Oyewumi, O. 2005. (Re)Constituting the Cosmology and the Sociocultural Institutions of Oyo-Yoruba. *African Gender Studies: A Reader*. Ed. O. Oyewumi. New York: Palgrave Macmillan.
Oyewumi, O. 2016. *What Gender is Motherhood: Changing Yorùbá Ideals of Power, Procreation, and Identity in the Age of Modernity*. New York: Palgrave Macmillan.
Yitah, H. 2006. Throwing Stones in Jest: Kasena Women's "Proverbial" Revolt. *Oral Tradition*. 21.2.
Yitah, H. 2009. "Fighting with Proverbs": Kasena Women's (Redefinition of Female Personhood through Proverbial Jesting. *Research in African Literatures*. Vol. 40: 3.

1 What Is Woman? Conceptualizing Feminisms

Much of what literature today calls feminist theory has its intellectual and academic roots in the political consciousness of the Western women's rights movements.[1] The narratives of these movements have been structured into waves and are woven around suffrage, equal pay, reproductive rights and other such issues that touch on women's autonomy and egalitarian relationships with men. Feminist theory as a body of scholarly works received attention and contributions from various disciplines that ultimately integrated their disciplinary ideas and approaches. This became a major challenge, as some concepts were used in different ways, perhaps due to the differing scholarly backgrounds of authors. This generated significant consequences for the methodological issues feminism is concerned with, to the extent that Judith Grant surmises that, "There is no one Feminist Theory. Rather, feminist theory is multicentered and undefinable" (1993, 1).

Feminism appears to have fastened itself onto one or another of many male theories with the aim of mitigating it. These attempts have resulted in what Grant terms 'hyphenated feminism,' 'Marxist-feminism' or 'psychoanalytic feminism,' to mention a few (1993, 1). In this chapter, while I find what led to so many different feminisms interesting, I am more interested in what led to another form of feminism: African feminisms. I interrogate (African) feminisms' many trajectories, as well as those critical concepts that underscore their theoretical foundations.

From Suffrage to Decolonized Feminisms

Not only have gender hierarchies and differences been fundamental attributes of human societies, they have also largely determined the essence and organization of human life. Pervading nearly every institution across diverse cultures, they intrinsically inform most considerations of what being human entails. Feminist explorations of the many effects of sexism supposedly started as analytical investigations of women's inferior ranking with respect to men. Inadvertently, it became obvious that there was indeed also a 'second classing' of women vis-à-vis women. This led to the emergence of 'woman' as a conceptual imperative within the discourse of feminism.

This inherent conceptual flaw articulated by Sojourner Truth, the African American slave and abolitionist, remains rhetorical and continues to resonate within feminist discourse. Truth's rhetorical question "Ain't I a Woman?" foreshadowed what would eventually become one of the fundamental questions of not just Western feminism, as Sharin Elkholy suggests, but indeed feminism across culture and discipline: "Who and what precisely is a woman?" (Elkholy & Sharin n.d.):

> That man over there says that women need to be helped ... and to have the best place everywhere. Nobody ever helps me ... or gives me any best place! And ain't I a woman? ... I have plowed, and planted, and have gathered into barns, and no man could head me! And ain't I a woman?
>
> (cited in Lloyd 2005, 35)

Truth's harangue made obvious the apparent difference and the ostensible racist notion that had become intrinsic to the concept of 'woman.' The existential nature of woman was set in a contrast of woman as White versus woman as African or 'of colour.' While woman in the White community remained fragile, frail, delicate and supposedly weak, woman in the Black/African community did not fit that usage. Like Sojourner Truth, Black/African women appeared to be able to plough and plant and gather into barns and bear the lash as well. Truth's symbolic question thus prompted this category of women to become the 'resistance' to what would have become a 'colonized' feminism by White middle-class women.

African American women's resistance to this colonized feminism became not just more conspicuous but forceful during the second wave of feminism. The poet bell hooks, in response to Betty Friedan's *Feminine Mystique*, revisited the controversy of what it is to be woman and Black, thereby extending the unfinished business of feminism's first wave into the next. Friedan's *Feminine Mystique*, frequently cited as laying the groundwork of feminism as a theoretical position, describes in lucid details the existential crisis which modern White women lived through who were stuck in conventional roles and with huge dependency on a male spouse. For Friedan, the "feminine mystique" was an unnamed problem linked to the daily domestic life of the housewife (1974, 25) since most of the women Friedan quizzed described this existential impasse in terms of their daily lives. Friedan reasoned that the solution for achieving economic liberty for middle-class White woman was paid employment rather than unpaid homemaking.

While economic freedom for White middle-class woman was tied to going to work, the choice to *not* work appeared a better route to freedom for the African American woman. Critiquing Friedan, bell hooks argues that "work" is indeed a White feminist notion and is consistent with high-end careers, referring in no way to the low-end or demeaning jobs reserved for women of colour, especially Black women. To hooks, White feminists were blinded to the experiences of other women, especially Black women, who were "working" but without job satisfaction and financial sufficiency. While 'Friedanian women' sought self-realization, 'hooksian women' struggled for self-preservation. The paths of these categories of women towards freedom from oppression and equality with men appeared totally different. The African American woman would have to first struggle to be equal to the White middle-class American woman before she could consider achieving equality with the African American man, let alone the White American man.

Understanding the peculiarity of their prevailing struggle – that their oppression differed significantly from that of White American women and perhaps that of women of other races – African American women felt they needed a new movement through which they could resist this new form of colonialism and fight the status quo which kept them subjugated. This subjugation went beyond the colour of their skin (explaining why white women dominated them) to the fact that women were being dominated by both White and Black men. Consequently, a new movement labelled Black feminism emerged that argued the interconnectedness of racism, sexism and class oppression.

Outlining the reason why sex prejudice prevailed against African American women, bell hooks saw it as a political arrangement which saw that coloured males, with the backing of White males, received the right to vote while depriving all women of that same right. This decision by White male Americans to stand up for Black male voting rights while disfranchising their female counterparts was, for hooks, how White men bared the profundities of their sexism, a sexism which at that fleeting moment in American history was even more exalted than their racism (1990, 3).

Although the struggle for liberation had been a joint effort by African American men and women, hooks posits that African American male political leaders maintained patriarchal values by coercing Black females to assume a submissive position which required them to run the home and produce for the home front warriors who were capable of a revolt. Inevitably, a patriarchal social order was enforced: African American women were relegated to the shadows of the private sphere, while their men gained the prominent visibility of the public sphere. A personal politic, one which was sexist in nature, got in the way, and as hooks notes, this was true to Sojourner Truth's prediction that "if colored men get their rights, and not colored women theirs, you see the colored men will be masters over the women, and it will be just as bad as it was before" (1990, 4–5).

African American women, as it appeared, continued to face these interlocking systems of oppression. Rather than deliberating on the adverse effects of these oppressions, White feminists tended to romanticize the Black female experience by recognizing the oppressions that Black women faced and in the same vein acknowledging their strength. The implication then is that although Black women are oppressed, they strive to sidestep the hurtful and harmful effect of oppression by staying strong (1990, 3); bell hooks contends that being strong in the face of oppression differs from surmounting or prevailing over oppression and that strength and fortitude should not be muddled with transformation.

The African American woman's stereotyped image as "strong"[2] not only dehumanized her, it also "became the new badge of black female glory" (1990, 3). The roles White women rejected – procreator, weight carrier and pleasure giver – African American women received applause for. Taking off where the White woman left off appeared to have been the lot of the Black woman. Accordingly, hooks notes that no one cared enough to discuss how sexism operates both autonomously of and concurrently with racism to oppress. White feminists could simply not prioritize gender over race.

African Feminisms

The reaction to the realization that Black women's perspectives were not adequately represented within the Western feminist movement, which consisted mainly of middle-class White women, was to create a version of feminism with the primary aim of understanding the problems Black women faced. Black women faced oppression based on their gender, class and race. They also faced being caught up between two movements – the women's movement and the Black liberation movement – in which they were othered. Being 'Black' was associated more with African males and being 'woman' more with White females. As a result of their invisibility, Black women sought to develop, through their own movement, a theory which could adequately address their peculiar circumstance of being Black and of being women. Such a theory would need to put a check on racist, sexist and classist discrimination by understanding the interconnectedness of race, gender and class. Ultimately, a fourth agenda, culture, was added to this list by African feminists who believed African American feminists did not integrate the cultural issues faced by continental African women. With the awareness of these inseparable and intricate social factors came the search for an intersectional theory amid counter theories.

African feminist theorists fall largely into two categories: declension and acclivity. The declension theorists claim that gender is alien to Africa and was transmitted via colonization. Acclivity theorists propose the counter argument that gender hierarchies and categories existed in pre-colonial Africa and that the prevalent power inequality only worsened in the wake of colonialism. Proponents of the declension narrative include Gwendolyn Mikell, Ifi Amadiume, Oyeronke Oyewumi, to mention a few. The acclivity narrative is defended by feminist theorists like Patricia McFadden, Amina Mama and Molara Ogundipe-Leslie. Since these two opposing arguments are the functions of different epistemic positioning with respect to Africa, they represent two different understandings of African feminism.

African feminism, saddled with the task of expatiating on the peculiarities of the African woman, generated a lot of *isms* in its attempt to decentre the idea of feminism. The general idea is that African feminism must denote a philosophically different attempt, not derivable from universal feminism, to undermine the oppression of women. This theoretical revaluation is thought to have commenced with Alice Walker's "Womanism" which aside from being a reaction to the consciousness that African American women's viewpoint were not sufficiently represented within the larger feminist movement was also a reaction to the preface 'Black' in the Black feminists' movement of that period. Walker's version of womanism was set to particularly tackle the problematics of class and race in White feminism and to enthusiastically oppose separatist ideologies. It is noteworthy to mention that Walker's womanism was not seen as African even though she touched on cultural issues which seemingly pertained to women in Africa such as female genital mutilation and the supposed ritual of tribal marking. Naomi Nkealah (2016) argues that womanism pertains to women of African descent who live outside the continent, not those who live in Africa. We see once again the incorporation of another social factor – the epistemic location of the subject – into the intersections of race, gender, class, culture and the extra baggage of conceptualizing the term 'African.'

'African Womanism' as proposed by Chikwenye Ogunyemi is a distinct and independent concept from Walker's womanism and Clenora Hudson-Weems' 'Africana Womanism,' although they have overlapping meanings. Ogunyemi intended to establish that womanism is widespread and to identify the binding features that Black female novelists share under this distinct praxis (1985, 64). Carving out a distinct praxis was important for Ogunyemi, who opines that "naming is power" (Arndt 2000, 721). Recognizing that Africa is vast and culturally diversified, Ogunyemi maintains that "for us, we cannot take the African American situation and its own peculiarities and impose it on Africa (ibid, 714). The "us" Ogunyemi invokes is suspect, however, given that Africa itself is not a homogenous whole.

Motherism, Catherine Achonulu's alternative theory to feminism, is grounded in the belief that the subtleties of organizing and structuring should be in collaboration with nature through all spheres of human aspiration. Acholunu perceives Africa as the model mother of the continents, the source of all humanity, and so an Afrocentric feminist theory must be anchored in and substantiated on motherhood, which has itself been a unifying factor of the Black race and pivotal to African metaphysics (1995, 3). In an interview with Nduka Otiono, Acholonu alluded to operating as both a scholar and a mother. This raises an important critique for motherism: are all women mothers?

Accordingly, one might also ask if all mothers are women. Acholonu asserts that motherism's thriving is based on a male–female complementarity which will guarantee the fullness of human survival in a stable and fair ecosystem. Complementarity then became yet another crooning for some African feminists, who seemed to think that the struggle to make woman equal to man must connote the hatred of men. Some, like Ogunyemi, argued that men are oppressed as well. But while we must concede that everyone can claim some form of oppression or the other, the critical question is whether there is one grand theory of oppression that covers different dimensions. Can there be a universal theory of oppression that includes men and women?

Obioma Nnaemeka gives a binary definition to her Negofeminism model: firstly, it is a brand of feminism that negotiates in a male-centred world, and secondly, it is a feminism that is egoless. Nnaemeka further states that the feminism she has observed in Africa occurs through negotiations. This form of feminism treads carefully, knowing how to go around patriarchal booby traps. It is enabled to hold talks with patriarchy in varied circumstances (2004, 378).

Clearly, if the tenets of Negofeminism involve engaging patriarchy in conversations, then they are a call to let the status quo reign. Negofeminism offers no clear strategy on *how,* since it assumes that it already knows. Advocating for gender complementarity, Nnaemeka contends that "[f]or women, the male is not 'the other' but part of the human same" (2004, 380), but then, the male has never been the Other: most of the time, the female has been the other. The essence of a feminist agenda, one would suppose, would be to "de-other" the female and equate her with the male. That, it seems, is when the sexes together will become "the human same."

Social Transformations Including Women in Africa is Ogundipe's alternative feminist framework. Ogundipe (1994) elaborates on what feminism is not, which for her includes parroting Western women's rhetoric. Feminism for Ogundipe does not seek to divide genders, separate races or split the struggle for liberation (1994, 221–222). Her account of feminism adds to the other approaches without taking us closer to any theoretical consensus in the African feminist articulation of the patriarchal realities in Africa. Ogundipe articulates the need for a range of *-isms* as exemplifying African feminists' efforts to conceive and authenticate their realities since the outside world was largely oblivious to the cultures of Africa and what it is to be an African woman. The patronizing and demeaning attitudes of Western women is indeed considered an alternative form of cultural imperialism (2007, 7). Susan Arndt raises an important point regarding this form of separatism within feminism:

> To my mind, it does not seem helpful to answer the ignorance and cultural imperialism of many Western feminists with the creation of a new term and the foundation of a completely separate or even separatist movement, while leaving feminism undertheorized as it is.
>
> (2000, 720)

Arndt posits that the call for separate brands of feminism has not defeated the Eurocentricity of Western feminism; rather, it has weakened our agential power as women, destabilizing our collective aim to call to question enduring gender relationships. For Arndt, "it is prudent to lead a discussion among various kinds of feminists in order to redefine it, rather than to split the women's movement by changing the terminology" (ibid).

Amadiume (1987) challenges the preconceived orthodoxies of social anthropology, arguing that prior to the colonization of the Nnobi people, gender roles and the biological categorization of being male or female did not necessarily coincide. Analyzing the political, economic and sociocultural concepts and structures of the Nnobi people, Amadiume exposes what one might term the fluid correspondence between biological sex and ideological gender in claiming that women could perform roles considered masculine or male dominated or categorized as 'male' if they occupied positions of authority and power; however, since these positions were not strictly categorized as masculine or feminine, breaking gender rules carried no stigma (1987, 185). The implication is that even though the flexibility of the gender system allowed women to reach statuses and ranks of seniority and authority, it also instituted a hierarchization that made other classes of women inferior (Nnaemeka 1991, 611). Amadiume defends this by upholding a utilitarian position that the empowerment permitted to some women by the flexible gender system had benefits that outshone the bestowment of inferior status to other women in the female hierarchy.

Invalidating the principle of relativism, which states that biologically, women are generally inferior to men in all human civilizations, Oyewumi (1997) argues that power depended on a person's positioning in the social edifice of age groups, not on one's biological sex. She maintains that seniority, not gender, is the principle that organizes families. A significant plank in Oyewumi's thesis is the relationship between *oko* and *aya*, which for her translates better as 'insider' and 'outsider,' in contrast to the western concepts of 'husband' and 'wife' because the position of *oko* is occupied by all the consanguine members of the household; hence, they belong to the family line and are referred to as the lineage owners – *omo'le,* in relation to outsiders or any incoming female, who is then the *aya*. The *oko* (the consanguine family) is made up of all blood relations irrespective of their biological sex, while those who fall within the category *aya* are conjugal. However, according to Oyewumi, the situation is different outside the family: the disciples of the *òrìsà* ("deity") were *aya* to the *òrìsà* (1997, 46). This is exemplified by the deity Sango, whose disciples are called *aya* irrespective of their biological sex.

Amadiume and Oyewumi, however, conceptualize gender differently. While gender is flexible according to Amadiume's analysis, for Oyewumi, seniority is the flexible principle. The connection between Amadiume's and Oyewumi's positions, an epistemological oversight resulting in a major lacuna in their theorization, is their inability to look beyond gender as bodily markers but more as performative roles. It is not so much about the bodies playing the roles but more about the roles being played. While the connection between roles that are considered gendered and biological sex was downplayed in traditional Nnobi society, the connection between power and gender was stalwartly established. This relationship between gender and power therefore calls for a detailed analysis. Underpinning the many definitions of gender are claims of supremacy, dominance, power and control by the One over the Other. Either as females or males, husbands (the one) are seen as superior to wives (the other). It is the epistemic significance of this position of dominance that often plays out in cases of oppression, and so we can talk of instances where women oppress women, men oppress men and nations oppress nations. I ask yet another fundamental question: what is gender? I will attempt to answer this question in the next section of this chapter.

Commonality and Difference in Feminist Theories

I have so far traced the historical trajectory of feminism, and how its preoccupations shifted from women's suffrage rights to its formation of a deficient universal theory which led eventually to its divergence. Despite the differences in feminisms, however, certain commonalities are fundamental to feminist theories, commonalities I identify as the underlying concepts of feminist theory. Having established 'woman,' 'gender,' 'oppression,' 'personal politics' and 'epistemic location' as critical concepts, I now seek to ground these concepts as principles underlying feminism, including how differing perceptions of them have shaped and will continue to shape feminist theory. This is significantly so because feminist theory is one vast field which has remained essentially transdisciplinary. I conclude this section by arguing that some African feminists have, through their superficial engagements with these concepts, misconstrued gender and misrepresented the condition and category of woman.

What Exactly Is Woman?

In the preceding analysis, I historically situated the woman question and established the analytical category "woman" as a fluid and political concept. "Woman" is fluid because its unstable nature deprives it of an appropriate definitional framework, and it is political because the idea of woman is often considered in its positioning against a dominant group, which in turn generates a power asymmetry. Notable examples of such intersectional positioning include the following:

woman to man – White women against the dominant group of men (both White and Black)
woman to woman (racial and class) – Black women to White women

woman to woman (cultural and class) – African women to African American women

woman to woman (intercultural and class) – African elitist women to African rural women

It is in this political sense that the concept "woman" becomes in Simone de Beauvoir's term an 'other' and in Gayatri Spivak's term, a subaltern. I consider the works of a few notable feminist theorists in this section, and going forward, I situate woman beyond biological essentialism and social construction theories towards a linguistic meaning of the concept from the lens of the philosophy of language.

Biological essentialism rests on the notion that a person's essence is rooted in the person's biology. Instead of examining the roles of cultural and social forces in constructing gender differences, essentialism contends that gender differences are established in biology or human nature. Essentialism is rooted in the metaphysical idea of Plato, whose dualist theory entailed a binary cosmology where the "world of forms" was ideal and fixed while the "world of appearance" was fluid. The fixed world held essences of the entities in the fluid world; for instance, there is a form of woman of which every other woman is only a derivative. A major implication of biological essentialism is that it takes as given that "things fall *unambiguously* into kinds, that the members of those kinds are all the same, and therefore the members of those kinds are unchanging" (Elder-Vass 2012, 124). Diana Fuss succinctly captures the problem of essentialism within feminist theory as "perhaps most strongly within the very discourse of feminism, a discourse which presumes upon the unity of its object of inquiry (women) even when it is at pains to demonstrate the differences within this admittedly generalizing and imprecise category" (1989, 2). Sojourner Truth's question, "Ain't I a woman?" resonates with this inadequacy once again.

Almost a century later, Truth's questioning is echoed in the contestations of Beauvoir (1997) on the assumption that the meaning of woman is explicit, necessitating Beauvoir's revisit of the 'woman question' in *The Second Sex*, thereby charting the path for the subsequent study of this conundrum by putting into focus the issue of gender. Beauvoir questioned the ontology of woman as *being* – whether truly biological essence made one a woman or if one *becomes* a woman through the numerous processes of indoctrination and socialization, consequently making woman a construct.

Constructionism, the polar opposition to essentialism, maintains that essence in itself is a historical construction and is susceptible to change. Fuss (1989) contends that essentialists often assert their opinions on deliberations regarding ontology, which is beyond the realm of cultural influence and historical change. 'Woman' and 'man,' for instance, are presumed to be "ontologically stable objects, coherent signs which derive their coherency from their unchangeability and predictability (there have always been men and women it is argued)" (Fuss, 1989, 3).

Essentialists make no concession for the historical/cultural production of the categories that foreground the recognition that seventeenth-century North Americans understood "woman" profoundly differently from how pre-colonial Africans did. While the constructionists posit that the natural is a construction of the social, the essentialists argue that the natural is inhibited by the social. Fuss provides an apt summary of this theoretical rivalry:

> the difference in philosophical positions can be summed up by Ernest Jones's question: "Is woman born or made?" For an essentialist like Jones, woman is born not made; for an anti-essentialist like Simone de Beauvoir, woman is made not born.
>
> (1989, 3)

Beauvoir's interest in the validity of the so-called woman question is exemplified in the historical advancement of White feminist theory in comparison with the challenges put forward by women who within the category woman had been othered and so felt sidelined within the movement. Rather than uniting women, the feminist movement seemed to be creating and recreating woman as "other." The concept of the other in Beauvoir's analysis is a very interesting one for feminist theorizing, as are analyses of the oppressions of colonized and exploited peoples. Beauvoir constructs her own dualist theory on a primordial existentialist notion of the self and the other. However, as with any dualist theory, a superior/inferior dichotomy is produced, with the subject being the One, the absolute, and the object being the Other, the inessential. Beauvoir explains this in relation to the man/woman dichotomy that woman "is the incidental, the inessential, as opposed to the essential. He is the Subject, he is the Absolute-she is the Other" (1997, 16).

Beauvoir affirms that othering is natural to human thinking. This implies that if there is a subject, there must necessarily be an object, and if there is a master, she cannot be master over herself but must necessarily be master over a slave. It becomes apparent then that no group ever appoints itself as the One without instantly setting up a subordinate group as the Other (ibid). Hence, the Self necessarily implies the Other. Though there are different attempts at defining woman, a common denominator to these different attempts can be inferred from Beauvoir's complex investigation into woman's situation: if woman is the necessary Other to man, then every creation of the category of the Other necessarily creates a woman, and every construction of the category of One necessarily creates a man. It is through these dynamics that our very existence is organized. Beneath these dynamics, however, are power relations through which gender is created.

Defining Gender: Essentialism, Constructionism or Performance?

Gender as a feminist analytical tool is complex and controversial, and its analyses are both numerous and contradictory, including the essentialist–constructionist debate. Essentialists not only emphasize the biological differences between males and females, as determined by oestrogen and testosterone levels, but also ascribe specific essences – fecundity, procreation and emotions – as essential to females, while strength, agility and reason are essential to males. These ascriptions, for essentialists, explain gender roles. However, since these roles differ across cultures, the essentialists' argument of universalized gender roles becomes weak. Biological differences are now popularly ascribed to sex, while the differences seen in social roles, behaviour, status, gesture, interests, character and so on are seen as entailing a person's gender.

The constructionists maintain that gender is created and shaped by the various principles guiding individuals in a particular cultural setting. Gayle Rubin (1975) considers gender the classification of the sexes forced on a people on social bases. For Rubin, the locus of the oppression of women is associated with her social life, and this is where the sex/gender distinction is applied. Rubin opines that while biological differences are pre-set, gender differences occur due to the imposition of social interventions which influence how men and women behave. In this context then, the gender discourse becomes imbued with relationships of power, with oppression itself being an exercise of power. Thus, the constructionist's arguments work vis-à-vis power theories of gender since it is this imbalance in relationships of power that has led to feminisms' reactions to the oppression of women. Outside of essentializing and constructing or structuralizing, I consider gender 'doing,' a performance. My deliberations in the ensuing paragraphs are on the views of Judith Butler and Sally Haslanger. The combination of both positions ultimately becomes a feasible basis for constructing and understanding gender in a new way.

In her book *Gender Trouble*, Butler presented a nuanced reading of the notion of gender beyond its limiting binary framework. In this work, Butler attempted to fuse the concepts of performativity and gender. Butler's notion of gender as performative is considered a rousing approach in feminist theorizing and alludes essentially to being a major text in the siring of queer theory. Butler contended that to argue that gender is performative is to claim that gender exists because it is performed (1988, 527), meaning then that "gender is always a doing," although not an act performed by a subject whom one could say pre-exists the act (1999 & 1990, 25). This simply means that nobody is a gender prior to doing gendered acts.

Building on the assumption that gender as a social construct serves to maintain the subjugation of women and also rationalize the persecution of homosexuals and queer persons, Butler's performativity of gender theory has been criticized by many including Eve Sedgwick and Dennis Schep.[3] In

What Is Woman? Conceptualizing Feminisms

Wenjan Xie's comparative analysis, however, Butler's use of the word "performative" appeared to have triple meanings: "the theatrical meaning of acting, dramatizing; its linguistic meaning derived from the verb 'perform' in the speech act theory, which is similar to 'enact,' 'embody' and 'do' and its extended meaning of 'citation,' 'signification' and 'reiteration' with poststructuralist modification" (2014, 20). My consideration finds the linguistic meaning most suitable.

Sally Haslanger's analysis of gender distinguishes between the physical and the social. She argues that gender cannot be based simply on structural, functional or natural differences; rather, it indicates disparities that are social between persons. Correspondingly, "[g]ender . . . is not about testicles and ovaries, the penis and the uterus, but about the location of groups within a system of social relations" (2006, 20). In Haslanger's opinion, gender is more about one's social status, the position one occupies: inferior or superior, subordinated or privileged. More important to the discourse at hand is the dichotomy between 'female/male' and 'man/woman.' For Haslanger, 'male' and 'female' denote the sexes while 'man' and 'woman' imply gender categories. She argues that one is either female or male because of some alterable set of anatomical features, while a person is a woman or man because of a person's positioning within a social and economic structure; thus, "one should allow that on this account of gender, it is plausible that some males are women, and some females are men" (ibid).

Following from this reasoning, if male bodies do not imply men, and females do not necessarily imply women, then physical anatomical bodies should not be the primary concern of the gender discourse. Gender is not located in the anatomical body; it is in bodies or groups. Haslanger furthers her argument significantly by differentiating between gender and race as a wider category:

> A group G is a gender (in context C) if its members are similarly positioned as along some social dimension (economic, political, legal, social, etc.) (in C), and the members are "marked" as appropriately in this position by observed or imagined bodily features presumed to be evidence of reproductive capacities or function.
>
> (2004, 8)

Similarly for race, Haslanger constructs the argument thus:

> A group is racialized (in context C) if its members are socially positioned as subordinate or privileged along some dimension (economic, political, legal, social, etc.) (in C), and the group is "marked" as a target for this treatment by observed or imagined bodily features presumed to be evidence of ancestral links to a certain geographical region.
>
> (2004, 7)

A clear indication that our social structures are hierarchical is the fact that social positioning places us as either privileged or subordinate along some dimensions. Gender discourse holds that men occupy the privileged positions and women the subordinate ones. In the analysis of de Beauvoir's proclamation that woman is the necessary other to man, I postulated that if the category of the Other necessarily creates a woman, then every construction of the category of One must necessarily create a man. Haslanger's (2004) assertion draws attention to the importance of both corporeal and ecological pointers; this means that pointers like 'Afro American woman,' 'Latino woman,' 'Indian woman' and so on, set against a privileged *White* woman, are also pointers to the construction of an 'other.'

These differing attempts at unmasking gender provide means by which we can arrive at some understanding of gender. In a significant sense, gender can be seen as "the masculinity of dominance and power (of the 'one') over the femininity of subordination and docility (of the 'other')" (Oyeleye 2017, 359). The masculinity of dominance is permitted to subjugate the femininity of subordination; gender functions consciously or unconsciously as the mechanism by which bodies relate. Gendering produces the visible disparities and inequities of class, race and sex. I could argue then that classifying sex, culture, race and so on along the lines of superiority and dominance, especially over others believed to be subordinated, implies gendering. Gender then serves as the means through which the constructs of the One over the Other derives.

Oppression

In arguing for a coalesced explanation of woman/female, Elizabeth Spelman (1988) identified what she calls the commonality problem. She questioned what could count as gender beyond bodily markers that are common to women of different places and times. Since feminism as a movement is aimed at ending the oppression of women, we work on the theory that all women are oppressed. If oppression is singled out as an enduring commonality to all females (Cudd 2006, 9), we are left to ponder what counts as oppression. Oppression must satisfy the following conditions: the harm condition; the social group condition; the privilege condition and the coercion condition (2006, 25). For Marilyn Frye, the first three conditions will suffice.

One commonality amid the different theorizations on oppression remains that oppression is multidimensional (Frye 2008; Young 2006; Cudd 2006). The word 'oppression,' for Frye,

> is dangerous . . . and endangered. It is much misused, and sometimes not innocently. The statement that women are oppressed is frequently met with

the claim that men are oppressed too. We hear that oppressing is oppressive to those who oppress as well as to those they oppress.

(2008, 41)

This makes oppression a double-edged sword. How oppression is oppressive to the oppressor might be unclear, but within the gender order, women who are oppressed include women who are privileged in certain aspects but take on the position of the oppressor with respect to other groups of women who are relatively disadvantaged (Bradley 1996, 93).

For Frye (2008), oppression takes its root from the element 'press' (42; Cudd 2006, vii). A thing can be described as pressed if it is caught between or among forces and obstructions which are related to the extent that "they restrain, restrict or prevent the thing's motion or mobility. Mold. Immobilize. Reduce" (Frye 2008, 42). Comparing the oppression of women to the condition of a bird in a cage – trapped no matter which way you turn – Frye contends that oppressed people live their lives in confinement, lives that are shaped by unavoidable forces and barriers: "You can't win. You are caught in a bind, caught between systematically related pressures" (ibid). An oppressed person is oppressed not because she is an individual but because she belongs to a group or class of people that is systematically degraded and constructed. Significantly, we experience misery and affliction partially or wholly because we belong to a particular group or class, and in the instance under exploration, it is the category woman (ibid, 44 & 48).

Iris Young furthers the discourse on the definitional import of the concept of oppression by reflecting on the situations of the groups considered as oppressed. She argues that "groups are not oppressed to the same extent or in the same ways" (2006, 4). For Frye, people who are oppressed face the common condition of having their abilities inhibited: to advance or just to communicate their thoughts, wishes, opinions, beliefs and emotions. Owing to the differences in the nature of the injustices members of oppressed groups face, Young suggests that oppression refers to a group of concepts, not just conditions, and she divides these concepts into five categories: exploitation, marginalization, powerlessness, cultural imperialism and violence (Young, 2006).

Following Marx's theory of exploitation, Young argues that exploitation entails the continual transfer of the results of one social group's labour to benefit another: "Gender exploitation has two aspects, transfer of the fruits of material labour to men and transfer of nurturing and sexual energies to men" (Young 2006, 7; Cudd 2006, 6, 96, 106). Africans, considered the other, faced gender exploitation as a group through capitalist super exploitation which considered them a source of inexpensive labour, an economical advantage to the Global North.

Marginalization, Young's second face of oppression, is "the most dangerous form of oppression. A whole category of people is expelled from useful participation in social life and thus potentially subjected to severe material deprivation and even extermination" (2006, 9). African American women were so marginalized that they became invisible, the Other not only to African American men but also White American women. As bell hooks notes, White women alongside Black men fall on both sides of the divide: they can assume the roles of both oppressor and oppressed. While Black men may be victims of racism, sexism positions them to exploit and oppress women. White women on the other hand may be victims of sexism but are enabled by racism to exploit and oppress Black people (1984, 15). According to hooks, "we are the group that has not been socialized to assume the role of exploiter/oppressor in that we are allowed no institutionalized 'other' that we can exploit or oppress" (ibid, 14). She takes for granted, however, that African women felt marginalized by African American women who had supposedly imposed on them the peculiarities of their own struggles by their inability to incorporate the cultural concerns of African women.

Powerlessness, Young's third face of oppression, is founded on the Marxist idea that class was a necessary tool for revealing the structure of exploitation and powerlessness. Although Young utilizes powerlessness to describe those dominated by economic exploitation, she neglects the view that the supposed powerless have power of some sort that can appear in the form of ignorance, a survival strategy subjugated people use to fight their domination. This form of power, often masquerading as powerlessness, is seen in the narratives of many colonized people. Marginalized groups, using powerlessness to their benefit, are often able to recognize the special vantage point their marginality gives them and can "make use of this perspective to criticize the dominant racist, classist, sexist hegemony as well as to envision and create a counter-hegemony" (hooks 1984, 15).

Cultural imperialism, the fourth face of oppression, involves imposing on a marginalized group a dominant group's knowledge, culture and worldview as the norm. Often, the dominant groups project their own understanding gained through their experiences as archetypes for the rest of humanity. The resulting effect on the culturally dominated groups often manifests as resistance, a breaking free from the constraints of the imperialist's ideals. This breaking free within feminist theory has resulted in its pluralities, the creation of many feminisms. This breaking free from imperialism also often results in violence, which while it is a form of oppression is also a necessary liberatory tool.

The fifth way oppression can present is through violence. Violence is a communal tradition, and its occurrence is not so much in the acts as in the social contexts around them. Young posits that "[w]hat makes violence a phenomenon of social injustice, and not merely an individual moral wrong, is its systemic character, its existence as a social practice" (2006, 13). Since violence is a social practice, the dominant social logic is that certain situations will demand and defend the use of violence more than others will; cultural imperialism, for instance, can transmute into violence. In attempting to assert its subjectivity, the dominated group may reject not just meanings, as Young suggests, but even the language of imperialism, as Ngugi wa Thiong'O encourages. Young intimates that the dissonance generated by this challenge to the hegemonic cultural meanings "can also be a source of irrational violence" (ibid, 14). Young overlooks the fact that there would hardly be any occurrences of imperial domination without the use of violence and therefore that its resistance or counteraction might necessarily involve violence of some sort.

Personal Politics

Largely a second-wave feminists' definitive slogan, the statement "the personal is political," was initially said to be a response to the political theory which polarized the 'public' sphere of politics and the state, and the 'private' sphere of the home. Challenging this private/public distinction, which defined politics in terms of civic life and the private or personal in terms of everyday acts and experiences like house chores, the family, sexist language use, sexual manifestation, reproductive choices and so on, second-wave feminists – through their consciousness raising – taught many to see these everyday acts as political issues. The term emphasized "the interconnection between public and private and suggested that politics could be at play even in the most intimate interpersonal relationships" (Grant 1993b, 405).

"The personal is political" highlights how women's everyday realities are not only informed by politics but also shaped by it and should conversely influence the political landscape. Sexism as a part of women's everyday reality is political because it is imbued with the politics of dominance. Thus, it was important to heighten women's political consciousness by encouraging them "to think that the experience of discrimination, exploitation, or oppression automatically corresponded with an understanding of the ideological and institutional apparatus shaping one's social status" (hooks 1984, 24). Defining feminine concerns in political terms, and in ways that emphasized group (meso-level analysis) as well as personal experience (micro-level analysis), would challenge women to enter a new domain where the apolitical would be left behind and a political consciousness would develop.

Epistemic Location, Epistemic Agent and Knowledge Production

In *Ecological Thinking,* Lorraine Code proposes an ecological naturalism that addresses the epistemic agent, the knower, as a "fully embodied, socially-politically-geographically located and living interdependently, societally, with others" (Lang 2007, 89). Code claims that neither knower nor knowledge can be separated from their habitus, which "captures the notion of an 'embodied history, internalized as a second nature and so forgotten as history'; yet it is also an 'active presence' evident in lived 'systems of durable, transposable dispositions'" (Code 2006, 28). Christine Koggel notes particularly that knowledge for Code "is constructed in ways that make people's location and circumstances relevant to accounts of what they can know" (2008, 178). Similarly, Linda Alcoff notes that "there has been a growing awareness that where an individual speaks from affects both the meaning and truth of what she says and thus she cannot assume an ability to transcend her location" (2006, 79). Although Alcoff takes a speaker's location to mean her social location or social identity, a person's geographical location also primarily determines the person's social identity.

This idea of epistemic location is at the core of many feminist standpoint theorists, most of whom opine that experiential differences are central to perspectival differences and that these differences in perspective convey epistemic consequences. Code kicks against epistemologies of mastery that reinforce the belief that dominion over nature can be exercised by humanity. More so, these epistemologies are indeed forms of coloniality, both physical and mental, that require delinking from. Epistemologies of mastery, to paraphrase Phyllis Rooney (2008),[4] were specifically constructed by (usually) socially privileged White men and women who were situated within particular networks of histories, narratives, metaphors, cultural assumptions and practices that worked interactively and ecologically together, rendering their accounts of knowledge as true and universal.

I think we can surmise that the privileged positions of these certain members had given them both the social context and the theoretical building blocks to construct from their experiences "universal" knowledges which they thought could speak for oppressed groups. In claiming to speak for differently situated others in third-world countries, Western academics created a dilemma for Others in our problematic postcolonial world. Considering this dilemma, Code opines that " 'we' cannot always speak for ourselves, yet people who speak for us, on our behalf or about us, are as often under informed, self-interested and imperialistic as they are supportive and empowering" (2006, 196). This again is evident in the trajectory of the feminist movement which I earlier traced. In speaking for the African American woman, the epistemic location in terms of social positioning of the White American woman as an epistemic agent reinforced the oppressions of the African American woman. In a similar vein, African American theorists felt that they were speaking on behalf of the African woman while increasing her oppression. African women in diaspora or on the continent speak as well from different epistemic locations of class, sexuality, religion, culture, race and much more to the extent that the crossroads at which these locations intersect might be too numerous and problematic for one model to resolve.

Africa is characterized by a cultural assortment that makes speaking brazenly of the African woman as a monolith impossible. Similarly, gender, even in its simplest form, as denoting masculine and feminine roles and characteristics, cannot in an African sense be considered universal; despite gender's fluidity on the African soil, a clear rule of patriarchy still reigns. Patriarchy, it seems, is an oppressive enemy, an enemy that requires a collective effort to fight. Unfortunately, feminist theorizing on the continent has yet to unify in its fight against patriarchy because we lack the solidarity and resources of the Hegelian Other for organizing ourselves into a "we" that demands recognition and that can sing in one voice. Obioma Nnaemeka articulates this position when she calls for the willingness to identify and endorse a mutual ground while regarding the distinctions that make the development of a monolith probable rather than the need of a monumental indivisible voice (1998, 3). An analysis on language use and how it has been employed in encoding the oppression of the African woman can become a mutual ground for the heterogenous voices of feminist scholarship to create a harmonious tune.

The historical narrative that has made Africa a third-world continent is tied largely around colonization. As a colonized conglomerate, Africans have been forced into the culture of the imperial nation and our remnant culture and traditional epistemologies destroyed. Despite African feminisms' inherent tensions, inadequate theorizing and lack of a coherent theoretical rallying point, it becomes imperative to suggest that one such unifying factor can derive from the need to decolonize feminist scholarship (wa Thiong' o 1981; Tamale 2020). African feminists therefore face two struggles – the fight against patriarchy and the commitment to decolonize feminist scholarship. Louise Du Toit explicates it thus: "African feminist work must . . . of necessity be unambiguously marked by a double resistance to oppression: it must do justice to the anti-colonial as well as to the female struggles against indigenous patriarchies" (2008). It becomes obligatory for African feminists, irrespective of geographical locations and epistemic positioning, to use the epistemic space of African feminist scholarship as suitable ground for the production of knowledge to the end of resisting our double oppression, decolonizing feminist scholarship on the one hand, which will be my focus in the next chapter, and patriarchy on the other, which is a major chunk of my consideration in the third chapter.

Notes

1 That feminism took its intellectual root from the West is, however, not an indication that its activism or advocacy for women's rights originated in the West.
2 See also Walker-Barnes, C. (2014). *Too Heavy a Yoke: Black Women and the Burden of Strength.* Eugene, OR: Cascade.
3 Sedgwick, E.K. (1993). Queer Performativity: Henry James's the Art of the Novel. *GLQ,* Vol. 1.
    Dennis Schep, D. (2012). The Limits of Performativity: A Critique of Hegemony in Gender Theory. *Hypatia* Vol. 27, No. 4.

4 See Rooney, P. (2008). Epistemic Responsibility and Ecological Thinking. *Hypatia*, Vol. 23, No. 1. pp 173.

References

Acholonu, C. 1995. *Motherism: The Afrocentric Alternative to Feminism.* Abuja: Afa Publications.
Alcoff, L. 2006. The Problem of Speaking for Others. In *Theorizing Feminisms.* Eds. E. Hackett & S. Haslanger. New York & Oxford: Oxford University Press.
Amadiume, I. 1987. *Male Daughters, Female Husbands: Gender and Sex in an African Society.* London: Zed Books.
Arndt, S. 2000. African Gender Trouble and African Womanism: An Interview with Chikwenye Ogunyemi and Wanjira Muthoni. *Signs*, 25(3). The University of Chicago Press.
Bradley, H. 1996. *Fractured Identities: Changing Patterns of Inequality.* Cambridge: Polity.
Butler, J. 1988. Performative Acts and Gender Constitution: An Essay in Phenomenology and Feminist Theory. *Theatre Journal*, 40(4): 519–531.
Butler, J. 1999 & 1990. *Gender Trouble: Feminism and the Subversion of Identity.* New York: Routledge.
Code, L. 2006. *Ecological Thinking: Politics of Epistemic Location.* New York & Oxford: Oxford University Press.
Cudd, A.E. 2006. *Analyzing Oppression.* New York: Oxford University Press.
de Beauvoir, S. 1997. *Second Sex.* Trans. H.M. Parshley. London: Jonathan Cape.
Du Toit, H.L. 2008. 'Old wives' Tales and Philosophical Delusions: On 'The Problem of Women and African Philosophy'. *South African Journal of Philosophy*, 27(4).
Elder-Vass, D. 2012. *The Reality of Social Construction.* Cambridge: Cambridge University Press.
Elkholy, S.N. n.d. Feminism and Race in the United States. *Internet Encyclopedia of Philosophy.* www.iep.utm.edu/fem-race/. Accessed online 8 February 2020.
Friedan, B. 1974. *Feminine Mystique.* New York: Dell Publishers Co., Inc.
Frye, M. 2008. Oppression. In *The Feminist Philosophy Reader.* Eds. A. Bailey & C. Cuomo. New York: McGraw-Hill.
Fuss, D. 1989. *Essentially Speaking: Feminism, Nature and Difference.* New York & London: Routledge.
Grant, J. 1993. *Fundamental Feminism: Contesting the Core Concepts of Feminist Theory.* New York: Routledge.
Grant, J. 1993b. Is the Personal Still Political? *NWSA Journal,* 5(3). Baltimore, ML: The John Hopkins University Press, 405.
Haslanger, S. 2004. Future Genders? Future Races? *Philosophic Exchange*, 34(1): 1–24. http://digitalcommons.brockport.edu/phil_ex/vol34/iss1/1

Haslanger, S. 2006. Gender and Social Construction: Who? What? When? Where? How? In *Theorizing Feminisms*. Eds. E. Hackett & S. Haslanger. New York & Oxford: Oxford University Press.
hooks, b. 1984. *Feminist Theory: From Margin to Center.* Cambridge, MA: South End Press.
hooks, b. 1990. *Ain't I a Woman: Black Women and Feminism.* London: Pluto Press.
Koggel, C.M. 2008. Ecological Thinking and Epistemic Location: The Local and the Global. *Hypatia,* 23(1). Stable URL:http://www.jstor.org/stable/25483157
Lang, J. 2007. Review of Ecological Thinking: Politics of Epistemic Location. *Paideusis,* 16(3):89.
Lloyd, M. 2005. *Beyond Identity Politics: Feminism, Power and Politics.* London: Thousand Oaks.
Nnaemeka, O. 1991. Reviewed Work(s): 'Male Daughters, Female Husbands: Gender and Sex in an African Society' by Ifi Amadiume. *Signs,* 16(3). University of Chicago Press.
Nnaemeka, O. 1998. *Sisterhood, Feminisms, and Power: From Africa to the Diaspora.* Trenton, NJ: Africa World Press Inc.
Nnaemeka, O. 2004. Nego-Feminism: Theorizing, Practicing, and Pruning Africa's Way. *Signs,* 29(2). The University of Chicago Press.
Ogundipe-Leslie, M. 1994. *Recreating Ourselves: African Women and Critical Transformations.* Trenton, NJ: Africa World Press Inc.
Ogundipe-Leslie, M. 2007. *Indigenous and Contemporary Gender Concepts and Issues in Africa: Implications for Nigeria's Development.* Lagos: Malthouse Press.
Okonjo Ogunyemi, C. 1985. Womanism: The Dynamics of the Contemporary Black Female Novel in English. *Signs,* 11(1). The University of Chicago Press.
Oyeleye, O. 2017. Feminism(s) and Oppression: Rethinking Gender from a Yoruba Perspective. In *The Palgrave Handbook of African Philosophy.* Eds. A. Afolayan & T. Falola. New York: Palgrave Macmillan.
Oyewumi, O. 1997. *The Invention of Women: Making an African Sense of Gender Western Discourses.* Minneapolis: University of Minnesota Press.
Rubin, G. 1975. The Traffic in Women: Notes on the 'Political Economy' of Sex. In *Toward an Anthropology of Women.* Ed. R. Reiter. New York: Monthly Review Press.
Tamale, S. 2020. *Decolonization and Afro-Feminism.* Ottawa: Daraja Press.
wa Thiong'o, N. 1981. *Decolonising the Mind: The Politics of Language in African Literature.* Harare: Zimbabwe Publishing House.
Xie, W. 2014. Queer[ing] Performativity, Queer[ing] Subversions: A Critique of Judith Butler's Theory of Performativity. *Comparative Literature: East & West,* 20:1. https://doi.org/10.1080/25723618.2014.12015486
Young, I.M. 2006. Five Faces of Oppression. In *Theorizing Feminisms,* Eds. E. Hackett & S. Haslanger. New York & Oxford: Oxford University Press.

2 Feminist Scholarship and the Politics of Language in Africa

The colonial legacies of the last centuries have left many third-world countries in an array of continuities and discontinuities. This idea of progress and incoherence is noticeable in all spheres of the lives of these countries, with particular emphasis on the framework of their scholarship. These continuities and discontinuities have, within feminist scholarship for instance, led to a clarion call, one of the strongest binding forces amid third-world feminist scholars and perhaps its greatest commonality: the undisputed commitment to decolonize feminist scholarship. This ultimately requires a deconstruction, a dismantling of existing structures of ideas, thought and concepts to achieve a reconstruction, a rebuilding or a reformulation of these in language. In this chapter, through the works of theorists like Fanon, Spivak and Mignolo, I interrogate how Western epistemological impositions have affected Africa's mode of knowledge production, suggesting Wiredu's conceptual decolonization as a solution to decolonizing thoughts, concepts and the *language of thoughts*. I also briefly analyze the philosophy of language, poststructuralism and the language question in African philosophy.

The Imperative to Decolonize

The imperative to decolonize feminist scholarship in the Global South derived from the need to move away from the canopy of a Westernized feminist ideal that kept third-world women – who arguably are not a monolith – under a Western gaze. What this Western feminist gaze implied for third-world feminists was not just that their ideas were not fully incorporated in mainstream feminist thought but also that 'mainstream' meant 'malestream.' Third-world feminists have thus become entangled in a matrix that makes them the Other while struggling with a corresponding failure to extricate themselves from the epistemological dungeon within which they have been forced by having Europe define who they are. Ngugi wa Thiong'o points out that our view of ourselves and our environment depends largely on our standpoint in relation to imperialism. Whatever it is we choose to do about ourselves, either as individuals or as a collective, requires that we unemotionally consider the effects of imperialism on

DOI: 10.4324/9781032706382-3

our lives. Our search for relevance can only be meaningfully thought out within the context of our struggle against Western domination (1981, 88).

The impact of colonization across Africa, and especially in the academe, necessitated a call for the decolonization of African epistemologies. Decolonization, a rallying point for third-world epistemologies, thus became not just a moment in history which saw the expulsion of the colonizers but a process towards gaining intellectual emancipation, without which there cannot be any form of liberation either political or intellectual. To achieve this requires a double theoretical requirement: the need to make decolonization a theory in its own right and the imperative of decolonizing theories themselves. This essentially is epistemic decolonization.

Decolonization as theory takes its roots primarily through postcolonial studies of third-world intellectuals such as Edward Said, Frantz Fanon and Aimé Césaire, as well as in the works of subaltern theorists like Antonio Gramsci and Gayatri Spivak and decolonial thinkers like Anibal Quijano, Walter Mignolo, Maria Lugones and Chandra Mohanty. Edward Said's *Orientalism* was a critique of the Western portrayal of the Middle East. His thesis suggests the existence of a persistent Eurocentric prejudice against the Middle Eastern people, their cultures and their religions. Through his rigorous scholarship, Said laid bare the orientalist's perspective which sees the Orient as the feminized non-European subaltern Other to the European (Western) rational and masculine Self. Thus, the *mission civilatrice* was meant to eviscerate everything the orientals considered a cultural heritage, and their very epistemological framework. It is the need to overthrow the burden of colonialism, for Said, that "culminated in the great movement of decolonisation all across the Third World" (1994, xii).

Frantz Fanon, in a similar vein to Said's discussion of the false Western perception of the Arabs, considers the 'childlike' primitive ways people of colour were understood by Europeans. He speaks to what, in psychoanalytic terms, one might call a schizophrenic split in the Black man's association with his fellow Blacks and with the White man, with the former being his reality and the latter a psychotic episode. In Fanon's words, "A Negro behaves differently with a White man and with another Negro. That this self-division is a direct result of colonialist subjugation is beyond question" (1986, 17). He identifies the problem of language as one that the Negro would have to face. For to speak a language that in this instance is the colonizers' language "means . . . to assume a culture, to support the weight of a civilization . . . [one] consequently possesses the world expressed and implied by that language" (ibid, 7 & 18).

Decolonization, for Fanon, is fundamentally a violent phenomenon. He considers both colonization and decolonization to be a matter of comparative strength. He affirms that

> [t]he starving peasant . . . is the first among the exploited to discover that only violence pays. For him there is no compromise, no possible coming

to terms. . . . The exploited man sees that his liberation implies the use of all means, and that of force first and foremost.

(1963, 33)

Violence is significantly a central feature of colonization. It was a weapon used by the colonizers on the colonized in implementing colonial oppression. The colonized therefore have a choice to make regarding violence, between enduring it – absorbing the abuse or transferring it upon the members of the oppressed native public – or seizing this violence and hurling it right back in the face of its initiators (Nicholls 2020, online). Thus, if violence is the language of the colonizer, the colonized must learn it as an integral part of the decolonizing strategy. I find justification for this in the theory of Gayatri Spivak.

Spivak illustrates the conflict between imperial nations and post-colonial worlds especially as it pertains to the representation of third-world subaltern populations. More importantly, Spivak introduces in this influential paper the concept of "epistemic violence." Michel Foucault had earlier developed the idea of the episteme[1] as the unidentified codification and edifice which defines the formation of knowledge of a given period. In other words, it is the systematic 'unconscious' structures which trigger the production of logical contents or knowledge in a particular time and place. For Spivak, Foucault had ingeniously overlooked how violent the production of knowledge through colonialism was (Bartels et al. 2019, 153) by his unquestioning assumption of the capability of the Western intellectual to represent the Other. For Spivak, "The clearest available example of such epistemic violence is the remotely orchestrated, far-flung and heterogeneous project to constitute the colonial subject as Other. This project is also the asymmetrical obliteration of the trace of that Other in its precarious Subjectivity" (1988, 288).

Let us reexamine the discussion on decolonization so far in the light of the postcolonial thinkers whose theories I have thus far considered. Said opines that the creation of the Arabs as a feminized Other against a masculine West was solely so that the West could subjugate the Arabs and foist its own language and culture on them. For Spivak, "epistemic violence is an integral part of colonialism as it not only undermines and dismisses indigenous knowledge systems by projecting European epistemologies onto the subjugated Other, but by also proclaiming Western knowledge of the Other as 'truth'" (Bartels et al. 2019, 153). This Eurocentric domination and consequent subjugation of former colonial subjects through its knowledge systems not only essentialized these colonial subjects as the Other but was indeed both a continuum and a continuance of the colonial system as neo-colonization. If, as Fanon and Spivak suggest, epistemic violence is a fundamental aspect of colonialism, it implies that violence is the language of the colonizer, and if that is the case, it must necessarily become an integral part of the decolonization stratagem.

The Western domination of the knowledge systems of the Global South also makes it possible for the latter to become vibrant research grounds

Feminist Scholarship and the Politics of Language in Africa 31

for data collection by theorists in the Global North, an intellectual version of the economic exploitation these third-world countries had experienced vis-à-vis colonization. Scholarship generated through these data is then used to sustain Western academia, which then continues to act not only as the storehouse of its assumed ownership of universal knowledge but also as the template of superior forms of knowing. Consequently, the West sustains and reproduces both its imperial power relations and epistemic domination through what has been called epistemicide – the brutal silencing of indigenous epistemes. Epistemicide, for Boaventura de Sousa Santos, "involves the destruction of the social practices and the disqualification of the social agents that operate according to such knowledges" (2014, 153). Since epistemicide is always with consequences, Santos asserts that unequal exchanges between cultures not only imply the death of the knowledge of the subordinated culture but also the death of the social groups that possessed it (ibid. 92).

Epistemicide, for Santos, constitutes both cognitive and political injustices that had endured since the commencements of the Euro-American colonization of the world. These injustices for Santos are interconnected and sustain each other. It is therefore logical to argue, as Santos does, that we cannot have a sense of global justice that is social without having a global justice that is cognitive. Thus, the challenge of this Western epistemic paradigm in all its ramifications should be both the justification and focus of a new critical theory and a new emancipatory practice. These new theories and practices, Santos asserts, "must start from the premise that the epistemological diversity of the world is . . . as immense as its cultural diversity" (2008, xix). Recognizing that we are culturally diverse should be fundamental to the formulation of alternative models of sociability and the resistance against capitalism. These alternative forms of knowledge are apparent in the various theories emerging from the Global South, and the most vigorous form of these alternative theorizing is structured by the idea of decoloniality.

Decolonial thinking maps the epistemic shift from the North to the South. For Walter Mignolo,

> epistemic decolonial practice arose "naturally" as a consequence of the formation and implementation of structures of domination – the colonial matrix of power or the coloniality of power – which Aníbal Quijano revealed towards the end of the 80s and continues to work on.
>
> (2011, 46)

Reacting to colonial powers as the producers of distorted paradigms of knowledge, Quijano suggests decolonization as an epistemological reconstitution. The quest for epistemic emancipation through decolonization in the work of Quijano was further developed by Mignolo, who also developed Quijano's conception of modernity/coloniality by reading coloniality as constitutive of modernity. Specifically, both coloniality and modernity are read as opposite sides of the same coin. While decoloniality was for Quijano both political and epistemic, Mignolo went a step further in attempting to differentiate decolonization from decoloniality. Mignolo saw decolonization as political and historical: he postulates that since the peculiarities of the force and the violence of colonization differed according to region, coloniality emerged as a common denominator to all colonized territories and peoples.

Mignolo argued, "Decoloniality is the exercise of power within the colonial matrix to undermine the mechanism that keeps it in place requiring obeisance. Such a mechanism is epistemic and so decolonial liberation implies epistemic disobedience" (Mignolo & Walsh 2018, 114). Decoloniality, as epistemic disobedience, is synonymous with delinking, a concept first introduced by Samir Amin. Amin's version was however formulated at the level of economic and political dynamics. Delinking, for Mignolo, must of a necessity be epistemic. Epistemic disobedience is thus an act of delinking from zero-point epistemology; it is a decentring of knowledge from its Eurocentric location. Mignolo uses an illustration that justifies this epistemic delinking:

> The vocabulary of any of the existing disciplines, words that denote the field of investigation or are concepts you use to approach the field, have two semantic dimensions. You will find, first, that most of the words/concepts you are using belong to European modern/imperial and vernacular languages and they have been derived from Greek and Latin. You will find, secondly, that most, if not all, of the words/concepts you use in your discipline and even in everyday conversation were translated and redefined around the sixteenth and seventeenth centuries in Europe.
>
> (ibid, 113)

The vocabulary of these existing disciplines taught and used in third-world universities is in itself a substratum for colonial epistemic domination. These concepts, texts, practices and theories have no basis in the lived experiences of their non-Western consumers and so cannot speak to the complexities and difficulties of their societies complicated, as they were, by colonialism. Africa, with its myriad languages, was further burdened by lots of foreign colonial languages and ultimately 'refined' through conceptual schemes that were essentially, in Kwasi Wiredu's words, "a philosophical deadwood." It is in this sense that Wiredu's call for a conceptual decolonization – a delinking of conceptual schemes from Western Eurocentric thought – becomes a critical decolonizing move for African scholarship.

Revisiting Kwasi Wiredu's Conceptual Decolonization

As earlier discussed, the Western domination of the socializing mechanisms of the colonized peoples – in this instance, Africans – instituted a colonial legacy of ideological hegemony which ensured that their existence and survival continue to be shaped by a perpetuation of Eurocentric ideas and practices. Colonized people witnessed a linguistic imperialism that ensured a continuous reconstitution of the dominance of the imperial nations to such extent that their realities and worldviews were not only expressed using these imperialistic languages, they were also experienced through them. The imperial languages became the mirror of their cultures. This is the kernel of the language problem in Africa.

The language question in Africa arose out of the disturbing fact that not only is the expression of our thoughts and realities achieved through foreign conceptual schemes but the collective fight against Eurocentrism and imperialism borne out of the colonial experience is fought using the language of the colonizers. This poses the problem of how a genuine African reality and world view can be experienced and articulated in a foreign language. Another angle to the language debate in African philosophy is a methodological problem arising from "the need to ensure that African meanings are not distorted in the process of analyzing them within the conceptual frameworks of alien languages" (Afolayan 2006, 41); some fundamental philosophical issues emanating from the West appear to lose meaning in an African context. Kwasi Wiredu argues against the universality of some Western philosophical concepts on the grounds that it is not possible to express them in other natural languages, such as Akan. Wiredu therefore calls for a conceptual decolonization in contemporary African systems of thought, aimed at re-examining its current epistemic foundations. By conceptual decolonization, Wiredu means stripping traditional African thought of all unnecessary impacts originating from our colonial history.

Through the critical project of conceptual decolonization, Wiredu is optimistic that the Western ideas which Africans have assimilated will be mitigated by careful use. His method for decolonization is that we attempt to delink a conceptual scheme or idea by translating such concepts from the Western language into an indigenous African language. If upon translation the concept is still intelligible in, and applicable to, the indigenous language, then it is not only worthy of further consideration, but it might also possibly bring to light fresh perspectives that might not have been possible in the Western language. Wiredu's objective is to deconstruct the avoidable epistemologies particularly of Western origin which may be found in the practice of African philosophy. His intention, according to Adeshina Afolayan, is that we construct an indigenous philosophy whose utility serves the existential needs of modern Africa (Afolayan 2006, 42; Wiredu 1988, 47). And this requires, for Wiredu, that we give reflective attention to a host of fundamental concepts around which human existence is built.

The existential condition of contemporary Africa has theoretically witnessed a rising in the activities of the once inaudible and perhaps excluded voices of the African female. So to Wiredu's non-exhaustive list of concepts requiring disengagement or delinking from Eurocentric thoughts, an AFPL adds the category 'woman.' Examining the woman question in African feminist scholarship, using Wiredu's conceptual decolonization, helps to untangle a conceptual and theoretical knot that makes it more intelligible in ways that offer decolonial perspective to the idea of woman. This is a task for the next chapter. A linguistic delinking of the concept of woman from its Western notion might be a necessary first step to the task of decolonizing African feminist scholarship. Prior to discussing decolonizing African feminist scholarship, and particularly how African feminist scholarship should be decolonized, I will take a quick detour into the disciplines of the philosophy of language and an African philosophy of language.

The Philosophy of Language, Poststructuralism and the African Philosophy of Language

The philosophy of language is an analytic investigation into the nature of meaning, reference, learning and thought, intentionality, and the relationships between language and its users and between language and thought. It is often contrasted with linguistics, which is more empirical than analytic. Although each field has its distinct features, they are interconnected. Linguistic philosophy is largely based on the logical analysis of Bertrand Russell, Gottlob Frege, Ludwig Wittgenstein and G.E. Moore, among others. The philosophy of language, also known as ordinary language philosophy, was largely a shift in methodology rather than a movement committed to critical analysis of the expressions of language, particularly those of a philosophical nature. Traditional philosophy and the numerous issues it encountered, like questions about knowledge, ontology, morality, metaphysics and so forth, are at a deeper level issues about language. Ultimately, the most effective approach to such problems will be to analyze the meanings of relevant concepts and propositions. These analyses, Peter Lamarque contends, will possibly establish the problems as spurious or can be explained by revealing overlooked or undetected logical or conceptual flaws (1997, 1).

The focus on meaning and language is not just a philosophical concern in the analytical–philosophical tradition; it is also largely a concern of the structuralist and poststructuralist schools in philosophy. Poststructuralism as a theory, or cluster of theories, is concerned with the relationships between human beings and the world and the practice of making and reproducing meanings. Its influence is, however, not only in the discipline of philosophy but likewise in a broader set of disciplines, including history, literature, art, politics, sociology and cultural studies. Poststructuralism is largely a reaction to structuralism as a school of thought which in its modest form is a technique of analyzing language, society and its popular culture. In a most dynamic form, however, it is a philosophy, a *Weltanschauung*, a worldview that offers an organic rather than an atomistic explanation of reality and knowledge (Palmer 1997, 2).

Seen often as a tenet that is at variance with the norm, poststructuralism, as a position that challenges the structuralist view, should not be considered a separate philosophy that subsists independently on its own and as a 'structure.' It should rather be considered as

> developing or arising only in response to pre-existing structures and, as a set of attitudes, helping us better understand, interpret, and alter our social environment by calling established meanings into question, revealing the points of ambiguity and indeterminacy inherent in any system, rejecting the rationalistic piety that all systems are internally coherent and circle around an unchanging center, showing how discourses are carriers of power capable of turning us into subjects, and placing upon us the burden of ethical responsibility that accompanies the acceptance of freedom.
>
> (Crick, 2016, online)

Poststructuralism, for James Williams, is seen as a

> thorough disruption of our secure sense of meaning and reference in language . . . of our understanding of identity, of our sense of history and of its role in the present, and of our understanding of language as something free of the work of the unconscious.
>
> (2005, 3)

In other words, for the poststructuralist, the language we speak does not originate from consciousness, and neither do the signs and symbols or images we recognize; they are instead the consequences of the meanings we acquire, replicate and transmit. Since communication is wont to change with or without intervention from us, we can make the conscious choice to intrude on and alter the meanings which our society presupposes. This work, following a poststructuralist agenda, chooses to alter the meanings of proverbs that denigrate women through a disruption of the linguistic status quo. Disruption – similar to violence, as I indicated earlier – is not an indication of something negative. According to Williams,

> one aspect of poststructuralism is its power to resist and work against settled truths and oppositions. It can help in struggles against discrimination on the basis of sex or gender, against inclusions and exclusions on the basis of race, background, class or wealth. It guards against the sometimes overt, sometimes hidden, violence of established values such as an established morality, an artistic cannon or a fixed legal framework. We shall see that this does not mean that it denies them; rather, it works within them for the better.
>
> (ibid, 4)

Works classified as poststructuralist are often not abstract reflections of theory. They are pragmatic or practical expressions of a given core – for example, proverbs – seen as fundamental and unchanging. Due to this pragmatic side of poststructuralism, its theorists

> must take a given actual structure and deconstruct it, transform it, show its exclusions. Thereby, they overturn assumptions about purity (in morals), about essences (in terms of race, gender and backgrounds), about values (in art and politics) and about truth (in law and philosophy).
>
> (ibid, 6)

This for Williams explains why different varieties of poststructuralism are given names that correspond to practical critical and creative activities, for example, *deconstruction* (Derrida), *genealogy* and *archaeology* (Foucault) and *dialectics* (Kristeva). Most poststructuralist thinkers also first sought to establish new linguistic concepts to describe their novel way of thinking and turned later towards articulating a consequent emancipatory critical theory (Hurst 2017, online).

The foregoing somewhat sums up an aspect of the thesis of this investigation, which is in part an attempt to alter language, particularly proverbs, that defames woman, and wholly to create a new rhetoric. My aim ultimately is to lay the foundations of an AFPL. In deconstructing, reconstructing and transforming demeaning proverbs, the aspect of orality that this work focuses mainly on, I intend that they become a 'counter-interpellation,' an antithesis and necessary intervention to the linguistic state of affairs. In constraining the old usage of these proverbs and transforming them, I expect that their ultimate meanings will embody a new interpretation and thus move towards transforming the everyday rhetoric for woman.

Returning to the initial subject matter, much as the concerns of the philosophy of language appear to be objective and thus universal, the language question and the subject matter of what might be termed an "African philosophy of language" differ largely from what is obtainable in the West. A major chunk of the discussion falls within the purview of what language African philosophy ought to be performed in, given the fact that Africa is linguistically and culturally heterogenous. While in one camp, there are those who advance the notion that African philosophy should be examined using indigenous African languages because the continued use of imperialist languages clearly indicates that colonialism is far from being over, a corresponding anticolonial act would be to jettison the Western languages for indigenous ones. Ngugi wa Thiong'O belongs to this camp. On the other hand, we have scholars who argue, like Ali Mazrui, that the proliferation of the imperial languages as global languages is a grand move on the way to achieving a universal system of amalgamated cultures (Mazrui 1974, 89). Beyond colonial languages being a blessing owing to their modernization and globalization allure, Mazrui argues that renouncing the languages of the imperial nations is more a step in the wrong direction rather than forward looking. He opines instead that some African languages could be optimally improved and utilized, thus cancelling out the need to renounce the inherited linguistic luggage of Western domination (ibid, 89).

Godfrey Tangwa suggests what he calls linguistic pragmatism, by which he means that the utility and pragmatic value of a language should determine and define our attitude and mindset towards it (2017, 135): "[t]o claim that an African cannot use a foreign colonial language authentically for self- or artistic expression or for knowledge production appears simply counterfactual" (ibid, 138). In a similar vein, Adeshina Afolayan, following Chomsky, suggests what he terms the "grammaticality of language," which he argues is based on the thesis that language is a neutral category that can be reduced to some general grammatical elements that find duplication in specific languages (2006, 55). Language for Afolayan is pragmatic, transactive and an output of grammaticality. Taking the argument further, he claims that for Wiredu, language serves this pragmatic–transactive purpose which enables individuals to deal with existential realities of a non-linguistic nature (ibid).

Afolayan (2006) draws our attention to the philosophical cogitations of Ngugi and Wiredu, whom he contends are both "concerned philosophers of language in Africa whose works approach the language question from basically the same direction but with startingly different conclusions" (45). Ngugi and Wiredu agree that colonialism is inexcusable and that our collective fight against Eurocentrism and imperialism must entail a form of decolonization. Ngugi argues for a decolonization of the mind; Wiredu opts for a conceptual decolonization. Ngugi advocates that for African literature to retain its authenticity, it cannot and should not be written in a colonial language. Wiredu advocates instead that it is not the colonial languages but the conceptual scheme we need to rethink in our indigenous language since we cannot completely undo our colonial heritage.

Following Ngugi's linguistic traditionalism, however, does not guide us against the linguistic traps and landmines in Africa's indigenous languages; nor does it guarantee that the contents of our thoughts will be decolonized or that the concepts we write about using our indigenous languages have been delinked from their Western origins. Wiredu's conceptual decolonization thus appears to serve as a golden mean between the two camps on the language question in Africa. This is so because it might not be pragmatic to write in our own indigenous languages since it will more than likely reduce the visibility of our creative and academic works as Africans, but a conceptual decolonization would safeguard us from carrying around a philosophical deadwood, a baggage of concepts which when thought out in our own African languages, lose meaning and become just another item of linguistic imperialism. This conceptual decolonization as an African linguistic methodology should be encouraged in disciplines across the academia and especially within feminist discourse in Africa.

Decolonizing Feminist Scholarship

Carol Boyce Davies begins her introduction to the edited volume *Decolonizing the Academy* with a significant assertion: "It is intended that the academy is perhaps the most colonized space" (2003, ix). The academy as a colonial structure, an "ideological state apparatus" to use Louis Althusser's term, was instituted to spread the colonialist ideology and ensure that the colonized would exist and continue to exist in a state of false consciousness. Thus, imperialist hegemonies have continued to prevail, with the academe being responsible for their continuous production and reproduction as means of sustaining the colonial status quo. This resulted in a privileging of knowledge emanating from Western scholars at the detriment of the indigenous knowledge systems of third-world countries.

The cry for decolonization has thus been all about decentring Western epistemological frameworks and recentring the indigenous knowledge systems of countries belonging to the Global South. As Spivak has rightly argued, Western epistemologies undermine indigenous epistemologies. The point therefore is the need for the revalorization and re-prioritization of the once devalued and neglected indigenous epistemologies. The appropriate space for this revalorization of the indigenous knowledge system is once again the academe. As Davies further suggests,

> the academy can also be liberatory space, a site of transformation and knowledge production . . . the sites from which contestations also emerge, new paradigms . . . deployed . . . "decolonizing the academy" must be an ongoing and parallel feature of any attempts to develop new paradigms.
>
> (ibid, ix-x)

Decolonizing feminist scholarship requires both a delinking from Western modes of knowledge production and a revisiting of the neglected sites of knowledge production (Oyeleye 2022, 101). It demands that we move beyond the academe as colonial space, where Western hegemonic epistemes are deep rooted, into the grounds for indigenous knowledge production, where local episteme can be mined. Building on the indigenous, for Claude Ake, is essential so that we can significantly advance Africa's development. This, he opines, must entail taking "African societies seriously as they are, not as they ought to be or even as they might be" (1991, 13). African societies cannot be viewed from any other lens but their own. Ake draws a distinction between the indigenous and the traditional, and he contends that "there is no fossilized existence of the African past available for us to fall back on, only new totalities however hybrid which change with each passing day" (ibid). This claim provides a leeway by which we can commence the reassessment of some of those totalities that undermine the worth of the African woman.

Obioma Nnaemeka also prioritizes the significance of the indigenous with her argument that "the work of women in Africa is located at the boundary where the academy meets what lies beyond it, a third space where the immediacy of lived experience gives form to theory" (2004, 377). This third space where lived experience gives form to theory appears to be located outside the academy. I opine that this third space belongs to the realm of indigenous knowledge produced outside the academy. For Abosede Ipadeola, "decolonisation must begin from the academy" (2017, 402). Reading both views together, I argue that there ought to be a continuum between the academy and the society to the extent that indigenous knowledge as lived experiences is extracted from fossilized oral traditions gathered from the society and rigorously reflected upon, critically analyzed in the academy and filtered back into the society. This extraction of knowledge from indigenous oral traditions, its filtering through the academe and its dissemination into the culture show an intimate link between the concepts of *episteme* and *doxa*, that is the link between knowledge and what one might call popular opinion. It appears as well that this dislocation between the academe where *episteme* is generated and the society as the domain of *doxa* is responsible for the disconnection between theory and praxis and perhaps the reason why feminist scholarship in Africa is yet to fully achieve its aim of transforming the society.

The greatest limitation of feminist scholarship within the continent then is its inability to gather *doxa* from the society, filter it through the academe as episteme and then return *episteme* generated in the institutions into *doxa* back into the society. Mignolo, in *Decolonizing Epistemologies,* identifies the nexus between *episteme* and *doxa* and makes the claim that " '[D]ecolonizing Western epistemology' is in principle a scholarly and disciplinary proposition . . . affecting both the *episteme* and the *doxa*" (2012, 40). By this, Mignolo suggests that "all of us who are engaged in decolonial thinking, decolonizing Western epistemology, and generating decolonial epistemologies want to have a transformative impact on public opinion, through our teachings and interventions" (ibid).

Episteme is a derivative of the Greek word *epistēmē*, which translates as "knowledge." *Doxa,* on the other hand, is a contentious term that is often contrasted with *episteme* and appears to be rather fluid. According to Takis Poulakos, Plato "placed doxa between knowledge and ignorance" (2004, 51). But then, Plato assumes that "doxa could be improved through education" (ibid, 53–54). In the view of Ruth Amossy, however, "doxa appears under various guises, such as public opinion, verisimilitude, commonsense knowledge . . . all that is considered true, or at least probable, by a majority of people endowed with reason, or by a specific social group, can be called doxic" (2002, 369). Doxa's force, Amossy continues, has nothing to do with Truth. Rather, "Its impact derives from its being accepted" (ibid, 317). However, from the nineteenth century on,

> doxa has reappeared under various, mainly pejorative, labels. It has been defined as a lack of thought and of style, as the vulgarity of common

opinion and the banality of worn-out language. It does not rest on materialist philosophy. It is a rather vague notion referring to what is thought, imagined, said in a given state of society. In this perspective, doxa is equated today with a set of other notions more or less closely related to its original meaning. The most famous of these notions is myth.

(ibid, 375)

Doxa then gradually begins to bear resemblance in some respects to oral traditions, like myth. To this doxastic list, we can also add proverbs and its poststructural postcolonial offshoot, 'postproverbials,' which I elucidate in Chapter 4. Postproverbials, especially in the context of the banality of worn-out language, serve here as a classic example of building on the indigenous. This is because prior to Raji-Oyelade's coinage of the term "postproverbials," these playful proverbial reconstructions existed within the Yorùbá society and were common knowledge. Raji-Oyelade, it seemed, had made a move to build on the indigenous by analysing doxa, as proverbs, within the academy and generating knowledge as episteme. This work furthers Raji-Oyelade's postproverbials through a feminist prism, that is, feminist postproverbials.

Through the medium of the feminist postproverbial, which I see as a momentous starting point for an AFPL, I will interrogate how proverbial language has been used to reinforce dominant patriarchal paradigms which mirror a colonial relationship. Beyond deconstructing these proverbs as sites for the indigenous roots of the inequality of the sexes, a more significant exercise would then be to reconstruct these proverbs to enable the African woman to discover her egalitarian standing even in everyday language use. This cannot be done without the necessary first step of understanding indigenously the concept of woman and its relation to man. This I will do, in the next chapter, through a conceptual decolonization of woman.

Woman, as an analytic category, is often wrongly assumed to be an already instituted, consistent group with similar activities, pursuits and desires, irrespective of class, race or cultural positioning or contradictions (Mohanty 2003, 21). However, when taken through a critical linguistic analysis, woman might no longer be the embodied universal subject that symbolizes the feminine. In instances where this embodied subject had symbolized the masculine as opposed to the feminine, Woman had been misrepresented as powerful, leading to such claims that precolonial African women were valued and equal to the men. Does language, set in oral traditions, reveal this as a universal truth? To put it lightly, who then is symbolized as the object who through language use has been demeaned, devalued and sexualized? It is important then that as feminists, and especially as Africans working within the expansive discipline of feminism, we pay more critical attention to the structures of language, especially sacrosanct proverbial language and how it has evolved over time as patriarchal. To produce decolonized epistemologies using our cultural insights, a necessary first step is to conceptually rethink woman using Wiredu's framework. We set ourselves this task of decolonizing the concept "woman" in the Yorùbá language in the next chapter. To achieve this, I will examine the female person as a metaphysical tripartite entity who is valorized in one category and devalued in another. The bracket where the female person is devalued is the bracket where, as the Other, she is womanized.

Note

1 See Foucault, M. *History of Madness* (2006) as well as *Order of Things* (1966) for further reading.

References

Afolayan, A. 2006. The Language Question in African Philosophy. In *Core Issues in African Philosophy.* Ed. O. Oladipo. Ibadan, Nigeria: Hope Publications.
Ake, C. 1991. Building on the Indigenous. *Wajibu,* 6(1).
Amossy, R. 2002. Introduction to the Study of Doxa. In *Poetics Today.* Durham, North Carolina: Duke University Press, 23(3).
Bartels, A. et al. 2019. Interlude: Epistemic Violence. In *Postcolonial Literatures in English: An Introduction.* Berlin: J.B. Metzler.
Crick, N.A. 2016. *Poststructuralism.* www.oxfordre.com. Accessed online 5 March 2019.
Davies, C.B. 2003. Introduction: Decolonizing the Academy: Advancing the Process. In *Decolonizing the Academy: African diaspora Studies.* Eds. C.B. Davies, M. Gadsby, C. Peterson & H. Williams. New Jersey, USA & Eritrea: Africa World Press, Inc.
De Sousa Santos, B. 2014. *Epistemologies of the South: Justice against Epistemicide.* London & New York: Routledge.
De Sousa Santos, B. Joao Arriscado Nunes and Maria Paula Meneses 2008. Introduction: Opening Up the Canon of Knowledge and Recognition of Difference. In *Another Knowledge is Possible: Beyond Northern Epistemologies.* London: Verso.
Fanon, F. 1963. *The Wretched of the Earth.* Trans. C. Farrington. New York: Grove Press.
Fanon, F. 1986. *Black Skins, White Masks.* Trans. C.L. Markmann. London: Pluto Press.
Hurst, A. 2017. *Post-Structuralism.* www.oxfordbibliographies.com. Accessed online 5 March 2019.
Ipadeola, A.P. 2017. The Subaltern in Africa's Political Space: African Political Philosophy and the Mirror of Gender. *Journal of Black Studies*, 48(4).
Lamarque, P.V. 1997. Philosophy of Language. In *Concise Encyclopedia of Philosophy of Language.* Ed. P.V. Lamarque. Oxford, UK: Pergamon.
Mazrui, A.A. 1974. *World Culture and the Black Experience.* Washington: University of Washington Press.

Mignolo, W. 2011. Epistemic Disobedience and the Decolonial Option: A Manifesto. *Transmodernity* 1.2: 44–66.

Mignolo, W. 2012. Decolonizing Epistemologies/Building Decolonial Epistemologies. In *Decolonizing Epistemologies: Latina/o Theology and Philosophy*. Eds. A.M. Isazi-Diaz & E. Mendieta. New York: Fordham University Press.

Mignolo, W.D. & Walsh, C.E. 2018. *On Decoloniality: Concepts, Analytics, Praxis.* Durham: Duke University Press.

Mohanty, C. 2003. *Feminism Without Borders: Decolonizing Theory, Practicing Solidarity.* Durham & London: Duke University Press.

Nicholls, T. 2020. Frantz Fanon. *Internet Encyclopedia of Philosophy.* https://www.iep.utm.edu/fanon/#H3. Accessed online 3 May 2020.

Nnaemeka, O. 2004. Nego-Feminism: Theorizing, Practicing and Pruning Africa's Way. *Signs*, 29(2). Chicago: University of Chicago Press.

Oyeleye, O. 2022. Feminist Postproverbial as a Panacea for Decolonising African Feminist Scholarship. *Journal of Higher Education in Africa*, 20(1).

Palmer, D.D. 1997. *Structuralism and PostStructuralism for Beginners.* London & New York: Writers and Readers Publishing, Inc.

Poulakos, T. 2004. Isocrates' Civic Education and the Question of Doxa. In *Isocrates and Civic Education*. Eds. T. Poulakos & D. Depew. Austin, Texas: University of Texas Press.

Said, E. 1994. *Culture and Imperialism.* New York: Vintage.

Spivak, G.C. 1988. *Can the Subaltern Speak*? Basingstoke: Macmillan.

Tangwa, G. 2017. Revisiting the Language Question in African Philosophy. In *The Palgrave Handbook of African Philosophy.* Eds. A. Afolayan & T. Falola. New York: Palgrave MacMillan.

wa Thiong'o, N. 1981. *Decolonising the Mind: The Politics of Language in African Literature.* Harare: Zimbabwe Publishing House.

Williams, J. 2005. *Understanding Poststructuralism.* Chesham, UK: Acumen Publishing Ltd.

Wiredu, K. 1988. Toward Decolonizing African Philosophy and Religion. *African Studies Quarterly*, 1(4).

3 The Dehumanized Woman in History, Philosophy and Culture

In examining some of feminisms core concepts – woman, gender, oppression, etc. – and interrogating the idea of decolonization and some of its underlying theories, Kwasi Wiredu's conceptual decolonization emanated as a necessary framework for African feminists to adopt in their consideration of the woman question in Africa. For African feminists to better comprehend the concept "woman," a delinking from its Western epistemic mooring is imperative. A reconceptualizing, through the media of African conceptual frameworks and languages, is equally important.

Following Louise Du Toit's (2008) admonition that works categorized as African feminism must be able to do justice to the indigenous patriarchies that the African female faces, and understanding patriarchy as an ideological structure which legitimates the rule of women by men and entrenches the oppression of women by men, this chapter provides a critical interrogation of the sociology of patriarchy exploring not just its supposed origins but its antithesis: matriarchy. I conclude the chapter with a metaphysical interrogation of the Yorùbá idea of personhood, touching on the ontological question about the nature of woman as being or becoming. This ontological unpacking allows us to fathom the tripartite categorization around which a woman is endeared as a girl child, disparaged as woman and valorized as mother.

The Sociology of Patriarchy

Patriarchy is described etymologically as the "rule of the fathers" or the imposition of male power over women. Its origin is often historically traced to the Stone Age, a period of prehistory characterized by primitive use of stone tools by humans, and through the agrarian and industrialized epochs. My critical investigation of the patriarchal structure requires examining the institution of family with the aim of establishing it as the basic mechanism through which patriarchy historically operates and sustains itself.

For feminists, patriarchy as a historical structure is arguably one of the oldest examples of exploitative societal structures in existence. It essentially refers to a structure of power that is male centric – economic, social, political, material, ideological and psychological – whose resultant effect is the oppression of women (Gardner 2009). Patriarchy denotes a worldview where men dominate, and women are oppressed because men dominate them. Kate Millet posits that "[p]atriarchy's chief institution is the family. It is both a mirror of and a connection with the larger society; a patriarchal unit within a patriarchal whole" (2000, 33). The organization of the family thus provides us the framework for analyzing the origins of patriarchy.

Like the arguments raised in Chapter 1 on essentialism, traditional perspectives on the entrenchment of patriarchy, either through religious or scientific frameworks, have considered the subordination of women as general, God ordained or natural, and hence undisputable and unalterable. The implication is that it should be held as sacrosanct, unquestionable (Lerner 1986, 16). Traditionalists working within a religious framework structure their argument around the Judeo-Christian creation story and conclude that woman is subordinate to man because she was created so by God. Arguing as well from the sexual asymmetry angle, they advance that since differing roles are assigned to men and women, especially in terms of biology, social tasks should follow a similar asymmetry. Motherhood was considered the primary purpose of womanhood, and those who could not be mothers were labelled abnormal. This is because societies' survival into the modern period derived from women dedicating a larger part of their existence to bearing and nurturing the next generation. As such, the division of labour based on sex or biological differences is simply functional (Lerner 1986, 17).

The explanation of sexual asymmetry provides a similar justification for female subordination located in biological factors attached to the male physique. Men's bodily structure, physical strength and aggressiveness were factors considered necessary for them to be good hunters. Women, as mothers, were deemed better able to look after their young ones and gather food for the family. The functionalist theorists Talcott Parsons and Robert Bales accounted for how gendered family roles may have been developed and maintained in the course of bio-social evolution. According to them, women's birthing and nurturing progenies substantiates the importance of the mother–child relationship and validates the assumption that "the man, who is exempted from these biological functions, should specialize in the alternative instrumental direction" (1955, 23).

This alternative instrumental role unquestionably places the man as head and hence equips him to dominate. If, as sociobiologists have argued, genetic factors determine human peculiarities and behavioural tendencies, then ascribed masculine features like physical strength and feminine features like nurturing ought to be seen as genetically determined. Thus, while women focused on duties termed emotional, men faced duties of provision. Should this assumption be true, it might be safe to conclude that the seeds of economic domination by men over women were sown from the prehistoric period.

However, Shehan and Kaestle (2009) argue that knowing for certain what the organization of the domestic sphere was like in prehistoric societies might not be conceivable. This is because feminist anthropologists and archaeologists have argued on the contrary that historical reconstructions of human life suggest that women significantly and actively shared the spotlight with the men.

Frances Dahlberg's groundbreaking work, *Woman the Gatherer*, a response to the *Man the Hunter* symposium of Lee and Devore, challenged the male-centred view which positioned women at the peripheries of societies while focusing on the endeavours of men as hunters. It also offered contentions on the female gatherer role, which entailed as much brainpower as hunting did. Dahlberg maintains that both men and women hunted and that men also functioned as caregivers. As such, roles were not specifically fixed. Antithetical to the belief that the intricacies of sharing must include a sexual division of labour, Dahlberg advances the contrary argument that what instructed each person to contribute to the whole was "a strong sharing ethics" (1981, 10 & 11). For Dahlberg, childcare was not an exclusive duty for women. It was shared duty! (1981, 9; Johnson 1988, 225). Sharing took place irrespective of subjective sex- or marriage-based responsibilities to ensure that both sexes had essential needs met. Sharing did not necessitate a gendered division of labour (Dahlberg 1981, 12).

However, the sexual division of labour became more conspicuous as societies evolved, and human survival changed predominantly from hunting/gathering to ploughing the land. Agriculture became a primary source of wealth and a move towards an increasingly sedentary human civilization. Since food supply in the agrarian societies outweighed what hunting–gathering societies could produce, this led to increased population growth, and the basis for this population growth was the invention of the plough as a fundamental technological achievement. Thus, the plough signalled an agricultural revolution.

This sudden change in the process of human civilization, from nomadic bands of hunter–gatherers to larger settlements of farmers, was seen by some feminist archaeologists to have been initiated by the women, who were gatherers. Margaret Ehrenberg, in *Women in Prehistory*,[1] surmises that since women did the gathering of wild plants, they would no doubt have been the obvious observers of the germination of plants, the experimenters in planting and ultimately the ones who would have been able to determine the best soils. Furthermore, she argued that they did the early farming themselves using digging sticks while men carried on with hunting. However, with the invention of the plough came a corresponding increase in male participation in agriculture because operating the plough entailed physical exertion, in comparison with gathering, which required less effort. However, tilling the ground required not only the physical strength of the male but oxen too. Since men's ploughing with oxen was more productive than women's hoeing with sticks, women's status was over time lowered.

Ehrenberg's work derives from Friedrich Engels' (2010) in significant ways. Engels, for example, alludes to the belief that within the family and in the society, males gained control because of the development of agriculture and that with society's evolution from hunter–gatherer into agrarian, private property emerged. Land had to belong to someone since it had become the major source of production. Animals also emerged, to use Engels' term, as the "instruments of labor" (2010, 106 & 117). With the creation of wealth occurring primarily through agriculture, more hands to increase production became a necessity. As Engels notes,

> The family did not multiply so rapidly as the cattle. More people were needed to look after them; for this purpose use could be made of the enemies captured in war, who could also be bred just as easily as the cattle themselves.
>
> (2010, 116)

With this social surplus came the increasing need for some to control more of the products of society than did others:

> According to the division of labour within the family at that time, it was the man's part to obtain food and the instruments of labour necessary for the purpose. He therefore also owned the instruments of labour, and in the event of husband and wife separating, he took them with him, just as she retained her household goods. Therefore, according to the social custom of the time, the man was also the owner of the new source of subsistence, the cattle, and later of the new instruments of labour, the slaves.
>
> (2010, 116–117)

Woman's biology as breeder and nurturer could also have meant that since more hands were required to till the land, more children would be desirable, particularly because life expectancy at this time was relatively low and characterized by high infant mortality rates. This implies that women had to be consigned to the task of breeding. Engels notes that mothers' rights were prevalent at this time, and "according to mother right . . . descent was reckoned only in the female line" (2010, 117). Mother right, indicative of a matrilineal descent, meant automatically that property inheritance would be passed through the mother, whom, it is assumed, was not in actual control of the wealth at this time since production was seen as a male duty and reproduction, female. If matrilineality prevailed, property as the earnings of man's labour would not be passed directly to the children; therefore a need to overthrow this matrilineal law of inheritance ensued. For Engels, the increase in wealth meant that the man's status in the family became even more essential than the woman's. This implicitly compelled the man to rebel against the established mode of inheritance for his children's sake. This was unachievable as long as descent was traced through the mother: "Mother right, therefore, had to be overthrown, and overthrown it was" (Engels 2010). For Engels then, patriarchy was established to kick out mother right and substitute not only a male line of descent but also a paternal law of inheritance:

> The overthrow of mother right was the world *historical defeat of the female sex*. The man took command in the home also; the woman was degraded and reduced to servitude; she became the slave of his lust and a mere instrument for the production of children. This degraded position of the woman . . . has gradually been palliated and glossed over, and sometimes clothed in a milder form; in no sense has it been abolished.
> (2010, 119)

Engels maintained the belief that the revolution which overthrew matrilineal/matriarchal societies and replaced it with the patrilineal/patriarchal order was by no means a difficult one: "A simple decree sufficed that in the future the offspring of the male members should remain within the gens, but that of the female should be excluded by being transferred to the gens of their father" (2010, 118). Asserting that wealth accumulation and its subsequent transfer was the reason for the creation of the patriarchal system, Engels points to how easy the American Indian tribes had accomplished this same revolution and only recently too. He predicted that subsequently other matrilineal societies would eventually be revolutionized and that patriarchy would become the ruling structure.

Engels attributes the development of the monogamous family to the same cause – the need to ensure that the true heirs inherited the property. Thus, in a bid to ensure that the wife stays faithful and to certify the children's paternity, Engels claims that, "she is delivered over unconditionally into the power of the husband; if he kills her, he is only exercising his rights" (ibid, 120–121). Engels' summation here positions the woman in an unenviable position of being dominated by the man, a position where she is bound to suffer oppression in all its ramifications. Clearly, if the society evolved from hunter–gatherer to agrarian and thus changed the social structures such as the family, then such structures must yet face further changes.[2]

As Western societies moved from agrarian to industrial, the very nature of the family changed alongside the evolving nature of work. Where in agrarian times, the line of demarcation between home and work was not so distinct, industrialization drew clear boundaries between work and home by simply but fundamentally moving work out of the home. Bahira Trask succinctly encapsulates this point:

> the movement toward industrialization was accompanied by a growing distinction between paid and unpaid work, a distinction that became increasingly associated with men's (paid) work and women's (unpaid) work. As

Western societies moved . . . towards a strong industrial base, the very nature of work changed . . . industrialization moved work out of the home. As the need for factory labor grew, men's work became more valuable and led to a societal discourse around naturalized roles for men and women.

(2010, 49)

Essentialists continued to ensure that the discourse was dominated by giving prominence to biologic variances between males and females. Once again, feminine traits of fertility and reproduction versus masculine attributes of strength and agility were highlighted. As such, the capacity to procreate became, for the women, persistently associated with the corresponding ability to nurture, while for men, strength and agility guaranteed their survival of the severe factory conditions of the industrialized society. Gradually, men came to be the breadwinners, with immense authority over the regulation of the financial management of the household, which "progressively led to women being pushed into the private sphere while men maintained the affairs of the public sphere of work and political matters whose end was to produce financial rewards" (Oyeleye 2020, 29–30). While men were seen as important and their productivity paid for, women remained unpaid for their reproductive abilities. Productive labour by man was ultimately recognized above woman's reproductive unpaid labour. This was the sociological trajectory that facilitated male domination, and hence the patriarchal order of the human society.

Matriarchy and Patriarchy in Africa

What has often been considered a major pitfall of historicity in Africa is the supposed lack of a written tradition before colonization. This assumption has serious implications for the task of reconstructing Africa's precolonial historical realities. Additionally, the general assumption is that African societies, like most other societies across the world, is largely patriarchal. However, Cheikh Anta Diop and Ifi Amadiume, among others, have attempted to place woman and the matriarchate at the centre of kinship organization in Africa. In this section, the focus of analysis will be on matriarchy, rather than patriarchy.

In "Gendering African History," Tiyambe Zeleza (1993) reviewed a considerable amount of literature centring on women, family and the economy of Africa. Zeleza observed that in the agricultural economy of Lesotho, women were involved in gathering, piggery, poultry, cultivation, harvesting and other household chores aside from cooking. He further observed that the increased adoption of ox-drawn ploughs changed the labour time; women did less weaving and home building and farmed more, while men took over home building as building in cut stone increased. Even though Lesotho's economic growth during this period heavily depended on women's contribution, women enjoyed limited political power (1993, 106).

The Dehumanized Woman in History, Philosophy and Culture 49

Cheikh Anta Diop (1989) argues similarly regarding the impacts and contributions women made in agrarian Africa as not corresponding to their political influence. Diop theorized that it was in Africa, the agricultural south, that matriarchy originated (1989, xii). Women oversaw the house and were also involved in agriculture while the men engaged as hunters. The strength and influence of the woman was determined by her economic impact within the social system.

The family system in Africa is somewhat different from the West. Ancestries in Africa are traced through a patrilineality or matrilineality, and one continues to be a part of the lineage even in death when one becomes an ancestor. While some scholars have argued that matrilineal societies are not necessarily matriarchal (Farrar 1997; McGee 2015), literature validates the argument that matriarchy is also consolidated through matrilineality. The discourse on matriarchy considers it a primordial family form that preceded patriarchy and is arguably older in Africa than other parts of the world. To aid our engagement with the concepts of matriarchy and matrilineal societies, I briefly consider how it obtains in some African societies.

The Akan people of Ghana are popularly known to trace their lineage through maternal descent, with property being transferred in like manner. Among the Akan people, although they are ruled by a king, the queenmother – *ohemmaa*, a "female ruler" – is said to wield true political power, so much so that she could, "under certain conditions, assume full control of central authority; she could become the 'king,' the omanhene" (Farrar 1997, 583). Tarikhu Farrar expatiates further that the Akans do not bar women from the Royal Stool; women have become kings in the absence of a suitable male heir.

Similarly, the Bantu people of sub-Saharan Africa are considered to be matrilineal. Rhonda Gonzales et al. (2017) proffered historical and linguistic evidence in support of the theory of matrilineality in their work on the *Bantu Matrilineal Belt*. In the worldview of the Bantu people, communities are perceived as being united within one womb. This shared metaphorical womb symbolizes a safe community with enough nourishment and food to feed the lineage. This is not necessarily because of an abundance of natural resources but rather, faith in the social capital of the lineage and their philosophy of resource organization and allocation within the community. This view bears resemblance to Dahlberg's regarding the strong sharing ethic which prehistoric hunter gatherer societies were equipped with.

An important feature of the Bantu matrilineal society is the bride service, which requires that young male suitors prove themselves commendable by working for the bride's family. The would-be husband's zealousness and virility are tested, and if they are found laudable, he can return to his matriclan with his wife and children, but if he is lazy or infertile, his bride service is terminated (although a terminated bride service after procreation appears to raise huge moral questions). Another important point raised by Gonzales et al. is the control of the labour of young prospective husbands. Since it was the older women within the matrilineages who had daughters of marriageable age, women of the matrilineage, especially in subsistence agricultural economies, wielded a great deal of economic power and prestige; that is, within matrilineal societies, *mothers* and *grandmothers* are essential to sociopolitical institutions (2017, 21).

Relatedly, Farrar attributes political power to women who are senior females of the royal family. Comparing the office of the queenmother in patrilineal Pabir of northeastern Nigeria with matrilineal Akan Kingdoms, Farrar argues that while "succession in the Pabir kingdom is contingent on one being . . . the daughter of a deceased king . . . Among the Akan, one must be a senior female of the royal family" (1997, 585). Farrar succinctly states the significance of the difference as follows:

> a Pabir queenmother, or maigira (literally, "female monarch"), holds her title through her filial connection to a former king; only daughters of kings are eligible. The Akan ohemmaa, on the other hand, holds her title because of her seniority in the royal matrilineage and not because of any relation to a particular male. The Pabir maigira is chosen by the king and his counselors. By contrast, the Akan ohemmaa was and continues to be chosen by her senior lineage mates, female as well as male.
>
> (ibid)

In my delineation of the matrilineal societies in Africa using the Bantu, Akan and Pabir peoples, I established that women wield both political and economic power. However, both forms of dominance were attributed to older females who were deemed to be senior citizens. Political power in both the Pabir and Akan communities was inherited, not earned; females who could become queenmothers were born into royalty. Considerably then, women's ranking and influence are better explicated by drawing the line between the majority of women – who as commoners did not possess power to any substantial degree – and the minority of noble and stately women who wielded political, economic and social power (McGee 2015, 5). This is a very important consideration for this work. Its importance cannot be over emphasized in my explication of the metaphysics of woman, a subsection in this chapter.

This analysis on matriarchy raises some pertinent questions. Does the presence of a queenmother necessarily imply matriarchy? Similarly, does tracing one's line of descent or inheriting from the maternal line represent a rule of the mothers? Farrar argues that matrilineality is often confused with matriarchy. This category mistake is because of the attempt by African scholars to redeem Africa's social and political institutions from the distorted views of Western anthropologists, a view which arose from the inability of (Western) scholars to establish a matriarchal society historically and ethnographically – one which could be deemed as patriarchy's nightmare, where women become cruel, vindictive rulers bringing both the family and the society under their domination. As such, scholars dismissed the idea that true matriarchal societies had once existed. "But also dismissed, and incorrectly so, was any notion that societies in which women possessed "real" political authority – authority that gave them power over the lives of men – had ever existed" (Farrar 1997, 582). In negating the assumptions of these non-African theorists, African theorists attempted to not only establish that African women in precolonial and ancient times held political power and assumed social statuses equal to men but also to suggest that this indicated the existence of a matriarchate.

Suggestively then, the presence of queenmothers did not necessarily indicate a matriarchy. In the three instances signalling a matriarchal society in Africa – Akan, Pabir and the Bantu people – women who were senior citizens and/or of the royal line had political influence, but this influence did not translate into political influence over men. The Akan were ruled by *male* kings; rulership by a queenmother obtained only in exceptional situations. The Pabir were clearly patriarchal, although their political organization accommodated queenmothers. For this work, I suppose queenmothers to be regents[3] – rulers or governors appointed to exercise power or function in place of the monarch in the absence of the monarch. Among the Bantu people, the bride service allowed older women a degree of power over men. He was, however, not obliged, like women are through marriage, to remain with the bride's family following the completion of his service. This was not an absolute feat.

Answering the question of how tracing one's line of descent or inheriting from the maternal line represents a rule of the mothers requires that we define matriarchy. At a most superficial level, matriarchy as the rule of the mothers is taken as the direct opposite of patriarchy as the rule of the fathers. There is, however, no consensus on the definition of matriarchy and on how mothers have come to rule. For Diop, matriarchy is not an utter or mocking victory of woman over man; it is rather a congenial dualism (1989, xvi). Diop's explanation provides a framework by which we can go beyond the spurious claim about the rule of the mothers to seeing matriarchy from the perspective of women's involvement in social organizations and kinship associations, as well as the achievements of numerous African queens (McGee 2015, 4).

In writing the 1989 introduction of Diop's *Cultural Unity of Black Africa*, Ifi Amadiume notes that, "[t]he 'natural' and social fact of the matricentric unit is basic to all societies, as symbolized by the pregnant woman. Consequently, the question is whether this basic structure of mother and child is acknowledged in social organization, culture and politics" (Diop 1989, xv). To advance this idea of the matricentric unit, Amadiume in *Reinventing Africa* defines matriarchy not according to rules of succession/inheritance as did Diop but based on the mother/child unit which for her formed the basis of a matriarchal system that existed in conjunction with a patriarchal system. What is clear about matriarchy in Africa is not so much a problem of definition but of the distinctive ways the mothers' rule. "Mother," as I will soon make clear, is beyond the mother–child unit as Amadiume describes. Rather, mothers, especially older ones, are a distinct female category worthy of consideration.

In concluding this section, I return to the work of Diop. He reiterates the point that patriarchy accompanied Islam and Christianity into Africa and hence is a foreign import. According to him, the progression within the African family is in the direction of a patriarchy which has been mitigated by society's matriarchal origins. The role played in this transformation by outside factors such as Islam and Christianity alongside the secular presence of Europe on African soil cannot be overemphasized (Diop 1989, 113).

Diop further observes that modern life is dislocating ancient structures and that among some tribes who have had little intellectual contact with the West, the matriarchal legacy still abounds. Citing the example of the Sereres, Diop observes that the son does not receive any inheritance, the nephew gets it all. As a result of such factors, it became necessary to change children's surnames from their maternal uncles' to their fathers' (1989, 114). In essence, Diop attributes these sociostructural changes to the arrival of Christianity and Islam as well as the Europeanization of African societies done through colonization. He makes it clear that although descent was traced through the mother's line, males still held authority, although not as husbands and fathers but as brothers of the mother – or, to use a European term, as uncles. Diop leaves us pondering as well if such ancient structures as the Sereres' still exist and if so, whether they will yield eventually to a modern structure and thus move to the next stage of their own cycle of evolution as predicted by Engels, who opined that subsequently, matrilineal societies will experience a revolution and patriarchy become the ruling structure.

Colonialism, like patriarchy, is a system of domination. It entails the political, economic, military and territorial sovereignty of the Other (colonized) by the One (colonizer). Africa, through colonization, experienced a distortion of virtually all of its structures – economic, political, social. Colonialism commenced due to changes in the mode of production in the West from the agrarian to the industrial, resulting in innovative production processes that replaced the earlier slave-based economy. While the trade on people as slaves provided a primitive labour force, the search for how to invest the amassed capital alongside the need for raw materials necessitated colonizing Africa (Ocheni & Nwankwo 2012, 47). Africa's political domination by the colonialists became necessary to reorganize its economy for possible integration into the world market, and its economic domination became necessary not only to find raw materials for the industries but to find a market for the products of its industries.

This sociocultural domination occurred through both European colonization and the imposition of religious values through the institutions and structures erected by Christianity and Islam. While Islam did not directly oppose polygyny, Christianity was in support of outright monogamy. Western anthropologists like Murdoch appropriated the nomenclature of an extended family on what should simply have been the traditional African family. The colonial epoch distorted Africa's social realities by erasing the existing lines of demarcation between our private and public spaces and remapping new ones. If the rule of the fathers had its own delimits within African societies, colonialism pushed the limits of patriarchy to sovereignty, an imperialism that mirrored the very nature of colonialism itself. The colonial epoch retaining its significance in our thoughts and acts thus left us with an heirloom, leaving us without an alternative as individuals, families and nations. This has in turn necessitated a restructuring of our world even down to our thought system, and this calls for a measure of reversal, a decolonization of all the structures already implicated in Africa's worldviews and self-views in the world.

The Metaphysics of Being and Becoming Woman

Metaphysics, arguably the foundation of philosophy, deals with the principles of things and is concerned with themes focusing on ontology, causality, identity/personhood, freedom/determinism and appearance/reality, among others. I focus in this section on first-order questions particularly the ontological status of woman among the Yorùbá of sub-Saharan Africa. I will look first into the nature of personhood, as it is against this background that my conclusion makes better sense.

It is worth noting that unlike other sub-disciplines within the broad discipline of philosophy which have related feminist fields, metaphysics appears to be inhospitable to Western feminists' concerns. Sally Haslanger (2000, online) attributes this inhospitality of metaphysics to the point that the fields of ethics and political philosophy have enjoyed more participation from women philosophers than metaphysics has. For Haslanger, it would be a mistake to conclude that feminists do not engage with metaphysical issues due to this apparent dearth of feminist metaphysics in the structure of the discipline. This is somewhat because the fields of feminist epistemology and feminist ethics have among their subject matter questions about the metaphysics of value, autonomy and the self. Additionally, the metaphysical discourses around essentialism/anti-essentialism, sex/gender, self/other, realism/social constructionism, etc. are clearly germane to feminist politics; hence, feminist metaphysics can be said to take place within the framework of feminist epistemology and feminist ethics (Haslanger 2000).

Witts, on the other hand, attributes this inhospitality to the subject matter of metaphysics itself, arguing that metaphysical issues do not seem openly relevant to feminism (2005, online). Witt's argument here, when read along the lines of feminism in a broader context, is true of many African feminists' theorization. African philosophers[4] have rightly observed that certain philosophical concepts when thought out within the African context seem to hold contrary to the Western view or appear to take a totally different form. Understanding this to be true also means that the supposed universality of some philosophical concepts is weakened when viewed through the African lens. Our understanding of the metaphysics of woman or the metamorphosis that occurs in the ontology of woman in African context particularly within the Yorùbá culture, is crucial to the thesis of this work.

Yorùbá Conception of Personhood

Personhood, in both the Western and African senses of the concept, is complex and contradictory. While the West discusses personhood in an individualistic sense, Africans conceive personhood in terms of the relationship between the individual and the community.[5] This communalistic approach to personhood inherently adds an ethical approach to the discourse (Molefe 2020; Oyowe & Yurkivska 2014). We can argue therefore that personhood in an African context has both ontological and ethical commitments. Ontologically, a person is more than a physical being. There are other non-bodily constituents, sometimes two or three that combine with the physical constituent. In Yorùbá ontology, *èmí* and *orí-inú* are the basic non-bodily constituents that combine with *ara,* that is the bodily matter, that account for the tripartite nature of human entities.

Personhood for the Yorùbá , like other African cultures, is thought to be acquired. Former Zambian President Kenneth Kaunda was reported to have once praised Minister Margaret Thatcher as being "truly a person." "Person," in this sense, is significant within the broader context of African culture as well as in the narrower context of the Yorùbá thought system. Kwasi Wiredu remarked on this that personhood is not a natural attribute of an individual; it is rather an attainment, the higher the feat, the higher the acclaim and glory (1992, 104). For Ajume Wingo, this understanding of personhood as a matter of degrees, is also a significant feature of the Akan idea of personhood (2006, online). "A person – taken in its fullest sense – is therefore an individual who, through mature reflection and action, has both flourished economically and succeeded in meeting her (often weighty) responsibilities to her family and community" (ibid).

The mature reflection and action which Wingo describes here has an ethical undertone which cannot be downplayed. Its economic variant carries with it the same ethical tenor which certain African moral theorists like Gyekye, Bewaji and Wiredu have termed an ethics of duty. Since mature reflection and its attending ability to not only flourish economically but be responsible in carrying out one's duty to family and community alike cannot be attained by a child, African traditional thought systems – and in this particular consideration, the traditional Yorùbá belief system – embrace the idea that morality is not an element we are born with (Oladipupo 2018 online). Thus, for Sunday Layi Oladipupo 2018, "it is arguable to claim that morality is not created by anybody but rather it is the community that gives this." This moral entity, equipped with the ability for mature reflection and action alongside the economic capacity to respond to her/his call to duty for both family and community, the Yorùbá denote as *Omolúàbí.*

Omolúàbí is the Yorùbá moral concept indicative of a cultured person with a sense of duty and social honour (Oyeleye 2018, 286). The concept, for Sunday Dada, is both normative and descriptive in content (2018, 266). It is normative because it serves as a prevailing code of ethics set by the community for its members and descriptive because it is not a self-ascribed category but one conferred on the individual deemed by society as worthy of this appellation. Olatunde Lawuyi (2018) argues that it is neither rooted in biology nor fixed by destiny. For him, "*Omolúàbí* is recommended to each person, as moral code as he/she grapples with the existence dictated by his personhood" (173). Lawuyi attempts to make meaning of the verb '*bi*' in the concept *Omolúàbí* as inventiveness or act of birthing. The verb undoubtedly puts the notion *ìwà* in the framework of evaluative, progressive human relations (2018, 174). This, in Adeshina Afolayan's summation, shows that personhood is merited within the ethical framework of the Yorùbá. It is a positive ontological procession, a moral advancement in time, from a mere entity to an exalted and honourable *omolúàbí* (2017, 886). From this adumbration, we can cautiously presuppose that personhood in the Yorùbá context is *a becoming* and not just *a being*.

Understanding personhood in the worldview of the Yorùbá is only a step towards our analysis of the metaphysics of woman. Oritsegbubemi Oyowe (2014; Oyowe & Yurkivska 2014) argues that the idea of personhood is gendered; it serves an ideological function, namely the perpetuation of patriarchy, and as such, it cannot be fundamentally considered egalitarian (2014, 87). Oyowe and Yurkivska (2014), in their work on African personhood, explore the relationship between personhood – in an African communitarian sense – and gender. They highlight three features which they claim characterize the concept, namely rootedness in community, the processual nature and the normative component of personhood.

Deliberating on the first feature, Oyowe and Yurkivska (2014) cite authors such as Menkiti, Wiredu, Tempels, Mbiti and Kaphagawani whose works have the common theme of giving enormous weight to the sociocentric view of the person. Regarding personhood as processual, they argue that personhood is a double-edged sword, passive at one end and active at the other. Thus, one is not born a person but attains personhood by integration into the society through the rites of passage (2017, 89). On the normative feature of personhood, they argue that attaining personhood is based on an individual's exhibition of maturity and their conforming with the rules that guide appropriate behaviour.

Examining the position of Ifi Amadiume on the notion of gender in traditional Nnobi culture, Oyowe and Yurkivska (2017) contend that Amadiume's argument, that gender differences need not connote gender inequalities and that the gender asymmetries observed in traditional Nnobi culture is indicative of gender complementarity, is faulty. This fault arises from what they describe as the enticing power of the notion of gender complementarity, which made Amadiume's elucidation of the data excavated from the Nnobi culture "blind to the recognition of the gendered and unequal nature of Nnobi" (2017, 95), the same way communitarian philosophers in Africa glossed over the way relational personhood is gendered. For the authors, a major flaw in Amadiume's work is that she takes for granted gender inequalities and hierarchies which have been profoundly entrenched in custom to the extent that she loses sight of them, condoning instead the traditional approval of male control over women. The roles of 'male daughters, female husbands' and its implication, laudable as it is, neglects the fact that it was not ever a rule but a rare omission from the conventional male dominance that was made available only to women of a particular class and affluence (Oyowe and Yurkivska 2017).

Motsamai Molefe, criticizing Oyowe, suggests that although Oyowe is aware of the distinction between the ontological and normative views of personhood; he does not, however, cautiously distinguish between them, thus making his conception of personhood ambiguous. With regards to the normativity of personhood, Molefe explores Carol Gilligan's care ethics as a plausible correlation with the concept of dignity in African philosophy, surmising that "[t]his view of dignity is gender-neutral and equalizes all human beings in terms of the duties of justice we owe to them" (2020, 73). He pushes consequently for a conception of personhood whose application to issues of gender should have resources for a social order that is just. Molefe's argument for gender neutrality through the idea of personhood appears utopian. Gender-neutrality truly *ought* to be the case, but what *is* the case instead appears to be what Oyeleye (2018) describes as a gender-relative morality where, in enforcing a communitarian ethic for the common good, people are accorded different ethical yardsticks as a result of anatomical differences, thus entrenching inequalities in moral standards (2018, 284; Ipadeola 2023, 125).

Becoming Woman: The Tripartite Nature of the Female Being

Turning to the subject of the metaphysics of woman, I begin with this question: *Is woman ontologically a being or a becoming?* I answer this question by borrowing Simone de Beauvoir's popular line: One is not born a woman but becomes a woman. Significantly, we consider the *female* person as a tripartite entity whose ontological reality takes her through three stages of being. Her *becoming*, the stage where she begins to significantly wield power, has often been erroneously ascribed as the stage of her womanhood. I argue on the contrary that this third stage of a female person's *becoming*[6] takes her totally out of the class of woman. She remains biologically female, but not socially woman. I consider each of these stages in the processual phase from girlhood to womanhood and then to motherhood.

That a female person moves through the stages of being a girl to a woman and then to a mother is not a strange fact. However, these processual phases somewhat ontologically define the female person. While girlhood appears the most straightforward of the three phases, womanhood and motherhood (which really isn't the best translation for the category which the Yorùbá call *ìyá*) are quite complicated and require unpacking. In doing this, I will investigate the nature of the female person from the standpoint of the Yorùbá and where necessary, will refer to other African cultures. My argument is that between womanhood and the supposed motherhood, lies a category mistake which has led to the confusion about the exoneration of woman as *ìyá*. This will account for the disparaging of the female person as *Obìnrin* and her exoneration as *ìyá*.

Amadiume considers the tripartite nature of maidenhood/virginity, wifehood/maternity and matronhood/post-menopause as phases in a woman's life cycle (1987, 70) and deploys the terms "female" and "woman" interchangeably. I argue that this confusion of the categories, especially the inability to distinctly separate the tripartite female person, is a fundamental flaw in understanding who/what a woman is in African feminist thought. Although Amadiume makes this tripartite categorization and claims, rightly so, that each stage has its own sociocultural significance, the question is: Do these three stages coalesce into being a woman? Who really do the Yorùbá refer to as *obìnrin*?

Oyewumi claims that the terms *Okùnrin* and *Obìnrin* do not translate, for the Yorùbá, as male/man and female/woman, respectively (1997, 33–34); she also uses the concepts "sex" and "gender" as synonyms (ibid, xii). This appears to be both a problem of translation and a classificatory error. Agreeably, mastery of a language is not enough in analyzing a foreign language to gain sufficient understanding that will facilitate an equivalent translation (Afolayan 2006, 48), so the obvious constraints of translation cannot be denied; however, the classificatory error appears to be a glossing of the sex/gender distinction. *Okùnrin* and *Obìnrin* will not necessarily translate as male and female in Yorùbá because the concepts *ako* and *abo* translate better as male and female. While male and female can be synonymous with man and woman, they are also distinct classificatory concepts which denote physiological and biological differences in living organisms and as such translate better as *ako* and *abo*.

The birth of a child is usually joyfully met with the primary question *ako tàbí abo* (male or female)? Notably, the Yorùbá acknowledge the difference between biological sex as a distinct category as opposed to the social category of gender as man and woman. Among the Yorùbá, female principles are generally held as symbols of coolness (*ero*) whereas male principles are taken as indicating toughness (*lile*). These accentuate the Yorùbá conceptions of female and male (Olajubu 2003, 9). Female principles are also associated with fecundity and fruitfulness. This categorization of femaleness and maleness is so pervasive that it becomes a categorization of plant and animal characteristics: a male dog is called *ako ajá*, and a male pawpaw is *ako ìbépe*.

Both phrases are also used in the deprecating description of a barren woman. On the other hand, the Yorùbá say, *Odún á yabo* ("the year will turn out female"/"May it be a fruitful year"). The Yorùbá therefore relate femaleness to fecundity, and this ascription is most likely a universal one. Since plants and animals are essentialized as male and female and they find expressions in the words *ako* and *abo* among the Yorùbá, *Obìnrin* and *Okùnrin* are only used in categorizing humans. Consequently, *obinrin* and *okunrin* translate better as "woman" and "man."

The Yorùbá generally refer to children as *omodé*. However, in distinguishing between a girl and a boy, they use the terms *omobìnrin* and *omokùnrin*, which translate as "woman, but yet a child" and "man, but yet a child." One could ascribe the ontological status of *being* to a child, and one could as well ascribe to the child the form of a male or female *being*. Normatively, and within the context of the community, s/he is yet to attain personhood. This is because the child is considered as "not having reached the time of the requisite maturity in moral thinking and social action . . . the child is not yet due for the test and deserves the kindest solicitude" (Wiredu 2020. online). As such, the child is at the onset of *becoming* a woman or a man. It is worth mentioning that at this early age of childhood, a socialization into gendered norms commences; the boy is cultured into being a man and the girl into being a woman. As they grow out of their childhoods, they grow into another stage of their *being*, where they become men and women, respectively.

For Keguro Macharia, girlhood in her indigenous Kenya was indeed a transitioning from one phase to another and often "through a ceremony (mambura) that created girlhood as a ritually marked physical and affective state. For instance, a karigu became a kirigu when she got her ears pierced" (2012, 5). In Macharia's view, "[t]hese ritually marked stages confirmed the realness of gendered configurations, created "real" girls" (ibid). My concern, however, is not in the affective, physical or ideological effects of these rituals of girlhood but in the processual stages within the African cultural context that signify the actual *becoming* of a girl into a woman. Macharia captures Wanjiku's testimony in Ngugi's story:

> When I was a child [of about eight] my mother began teaching me about how I should behave around men . . . When I got a little older, about fourteen, my ears were pierced – meaning that I had bought a new stage of maturity with the holes in my ears. . . . Then when I showed the first signs of growing breasts – before I had my first menstruation – preparations were made for irua.
>
> (wa Thiong' o, N in Macharia 2012, 6)

For the Gikuyu of Kenya, *irua* (circumcision) is an important ritual which connotes a child's passage into adulthood alongside other socially important values and expectations of responsibility. The rite of passage is a central feature in most African societies. The Bantu, as Gonzales et al. described, started female initiation ceremonies "at a young girl's first menstruation and a final ceremony was celebrated when she felt the movement of her first child" (2017, 23). Olajubu succinctly explains this rite of passage among the Yorùbá:

> Puberty rites among the Yoruba are either situated in the institution of marriage or lead to it. Popularly referred to as *becoming* a man or woman (O d'okunrin/obinrin), these rites mark the moment at which an individual attains a status of responsibility. . . . Of special concern to this work is what it means for a Yoruba female to *become* a woman [*d'obinrin*]. This almost always occurs on the occasion of the girl's wedding, which is usually post-menstrual. The Yoruba perceive menstruation as the conveyor of potential life and by extension, power.
>
> (2003, 95)

From the foregoing then, a girl becomes *d'obinrin* at puberty/post-menstruation. Menstruation is enshrouded in mystery, and in the Yorùbá thought system, menses is a contaminant, something that desecrates and diminishes spiritual energies but also a channel of power because it carries potential life (Olajubu 2003). It is therefore isolated from other energy sources to prevent spiritual energy clashes which may give explosive outcomes (Olajubu 2003, 92). Owing to menstruation's repute as a vehicle of power, Oyeronke Olademo contends that whatever restriction it is subjected to is out of reverence, not an assumed contagion ascribed to it (2010, 201). For Olajubu, however, who again viewed menses as a contaminant, "[t]he salient point here is that menstrual blood is labeled continuous not by the women who experience it but by men, who do not menstruate" (2003, 61). Mary Nyangweso Wangila further argues,

> Although taboos about seclusion of menstruating women are a way of acknowledging the maternal principle that women possess as producers of life, the ambivalence associated with menstruation as an impurity raises questions. In most communities, a menstruating woman is believed to be in a state of negativity, possessing destructive spirits – spirits that are not only harmful to men, rulers, and land, but to women themselves as well. The association of the women in this natural state with destruction and their exclusion from participation in rituals speaks to the defiling/purity category that is behind male dominance ideology.
>
> (2010, 312)

Becoming a woman appears therefore to be fundamentally attached to biology, and particularly to a woman's ability to reproduce. This could be because it enables the female person, now a woman in puberty, to move to the next stage of becoming *iyá*, which is by far the most difficult, in terms of analysis, of the concepts involved in the processual phases of femininity. This is largely because it linguistically implies, on the one hand, the biological possibility of becoming a mother and on the other, it symbolizes power and the ability to dominate. However, before I explore this, it is important that I reopen Engel's discussion, this time his exploration of the interlinkage between woman's reproductive and productive capabilities. Understanding production and reproduction in the light of Marx and Engels' analysis and why certain feminists' see the relationship between the two concepts as a reason for the perpetuation of woman's subordination, becomes imperative for us at this point.

The foundations of human society and the means to comprehending its history as well as its future, according to Marx's historical materialism, rest on producing and reproducing material life. The sub-structure of any society lies in a cooperative act of production, the production of material life itself. This first historical act "is conscious and planned, and it changes over time, setting in motion the complex processes of economic, social, political and ideological development that constitute human history" (Bryson 2005, 127). "Marxist economic theory argues that, under the historically specific conditions of capitalism, the only form of work that is technically 'productive' is paid work exchanged in the labour market for money and from which surplus value is extracted" (Bryson 2005, 129). While this largely leaves out the unpaid wages of women's everyday household toil, the female process of human reproduction and family formation is included in the latter definition of the concept of production. In reiterating the materialist conception of this process, Engels argues that "the determining factor in history is, in the final instance, *the production and reproduction* of immediate life" (2010, 35–36).[7]

Reproduction in Marxist theories is not only equated with biological procreation but also used to "refer to the broader reproduction of the labour force on a daily as well as a generational basis . . . [and] the processes through which the economy 'reproduces itself,' yielding inputs for future production and consumption" (Bryson 2005, 130). These shifting meanings obscure the demarcation between production and reproduction, and feminist theorists have wondered if there is any difference between the two concepts. Paltasingh and Lingam, for instance, argued that "[e]very act of production is necessarily, at the same time, an act of social and economic reproduction" (2014, 48). According to them, the difference between patriarchal households and capitalist firms should not be denoted on the basis that the household is reproduction's primary place while production belongs to the firms. On the contrary, both are productive and reproductive organizations: "The social and economic reproduction that takes place in the household could not have happened without the production that takes place at the same household. Likewise, capitalist production would be impossible without capitalist reproduction" (Paltasingh & Lingam 2014, 48). In their view, the supposed differences between work that is productive and work that is reproductive are essentially incorrect.

We can now contextualize the analysis. In traditional Yorùbá societies, productive labour – in the Marxist capitalist sense of work done in exchange

The Dehumanized Woman in History, Philosophy and Culture 61

for money – begins quite early for the female person. This commences from learning and helping in the family's line of production (often, lineages have identifiable professions or skills which they are known for) to general household chores (which begin to fall into reproductive labour). By the time the girl transits from girlhood to womanhood, with the onset of menstruation, productive and reproductive labour truly become indistinguishable. This is because she is ready for both economic productive labour and procreant labour. From this point on, her quest for self-actualization becomes obscure; she is heavily bound by cultural norms and values – a communitarian ethic of duty – towards her husband (considered her lord), her children (considered her future) and the attainment of personhood as culture demands. Her life aspiration is measured largely in terms of how she excels in her ethics of care towards her lord and her children, and her home in general. These communitarian and care ethics submerge perhaps every ethic of right to her individuality.

This equivalently is the point where *obìnrin* becomes a gendered construct and where as *obìnrin* the female person is most devalued, denigrated and disparaged. Almost like the biblical sheep before its shearers, she must remain dumb and possess instead a strong ability to endure the sufferings of being woman. It is only after her dutiful endurance of existential and communal sufferings (*ìyà*) as "woman" and as mother – the giver of life and nurturer of child – that she then attains the status of *Mother* (*Ìyá*)[8] – a revered term often used for post-menopausal female persons. The category mistake has often been in the stance of not differentiating between the female person's processual phases into becoming *Ìyá* – the revered one. Thus, this female person who has seemingly fought and conquered her battles is confused with the category of *obìnrin* as *ìyá*, who is instead a young procreating female person, still on the battlefield fighting towards actualizing personhood. I will return to this issue shortly.

I am arguing that motherhood, as an ideological structure and an idolized status, does not fall in the sphere of womanhood, even though it is coextensive with it. This argument enables me to wade through African feminist thought and interrogate the conflation of womanhood with motherhood. Next, I will explore, through African religion, the metaphysical status and powers of the institution of *Ìyá*. Oyewumi Oyeronke (1997) brilliantly argues that seniority, rather than gender, is the primary organizing principle among the Yorùbá. The import of her argument here is, however, not on seniority's opposition to gender but its significance as it relates to the concept of *Ìyá*. Used in sociolinguistic terms, *Ìyá* denotes 1) a mother, 2) a female senior citizen, and/or a female person who is in a high-ranking position either by virtue of birth or marriage into a royal lineage and 3) the possession of a sociospiritual ability (which also can invariably derive from the first two).

Being a mother in the first instance is quite straightforward. It simply entails the ability to procreate. Being a female senior citizen is equally explicit enough and is often populated by post-menopausal women and women of status or high birth. Thus, the office of the queenmother among the Akan, as earlier explicated, was only available to senior females of the clan. Among the Pabirs, eligibility to the status was based on being the daughter of a deceased king, and with the Bantus, older women's prestige was because of their economic prowess. The arguments which sought to grant social, economic and political power to African women were, in the view of McGee, based only on a minority of royal women (2015, 4). By virtue of their status – socially, politically, economically – these female persons had achieved personhood, and so they can be and are referred to as *Ìyá*. This can occur without them being biologically able to procreate.

In *What Gender is Motherhood?* Oyewumi notes that "Ìyá is not merely a body since the spiritual understanding of their identity is paramount in the Yorùbá construction" (2016, 70; Popoola 2022, 249). This sociospiritual institution consists of the mothers in the third denotation. In Yorùbá traditional thought, the concept is shrouded in secrecy and associated with indescribable mystical powers. They are referred to as *Ìyà mi,* and this can be described as the cult of the mothers. The *odu* Òseètúrá exemplifies this sociospiritual institution better.

The *odu* Òseètúrá in the Ifá corpus narrates the story of Òsun, a primordial deity who, among the deities sent on a mission to Earth, was excluded by the other sixteen male deities on the account that she was female. Òsun's reaction was to gather other female inhabitants of the Earth and form the *Ìyà mi* cult. The cult of *Ìyà mi* is also often regarded as that of *Àjé* and often mistranslated into English as "witches." Teresa Washington (2005) describes the females in the cult of *Àjé* as having many noteworthy attributes and responsibilities in society. Females who are *Àjé* are known to be endowed with mystical powers, supernatural abilities and the power to speak wishes into being which is known as *àse,* among the Yorùbá (2005, 14). Furthermore, she claims that "[h]olistic healing is an important aspect of *Àjé,* and its wielders use their incomparable knowledge and ownership of flora and fauna to create nourishment, healing elixirs, and poisons" (Washington 2005). While it might be contentious to claim, as Washington does, that "Yoruba females of all ages have some degree of *Àjé,*" it is a widely held belief that "*elderly* women, endowed with wisdom that is tempered by life's vicissitudes, are considered the most evolved, balanced, and powerful" (2005, 15). One dimension of what Washington regards as life's vicissitudes involves the changes and variations which unravel in the course of a female person's processual movement from girlhood through womanhood to "motherhood" in an attempt to achieve personhood.

Gendered Notions in Some Yorùbá Oral Traditions

I have attempted to advance what I have termed the sociology of patriarchy, which traces the historical trajectory of patriarchy from the stone ages of hunter–gatherer societies through the agrarian and into the industrialist epoch in both the West and Africa. In the African context especially, the polar concept of matriarchy threw more light on the supposed political, economic and social status of African women. Through Farrar's work on queenmothering, the privileging of senior female persons became apparent, which necessitated that we attempt to understand what it takes for a female person to achieve personhood in the African context.

In my analysis, a woman is regarded as being and becoming in the understanding of personhood in its normative and ontological meaning. In attaining personhood, an assumed fulfilment of an individual's *being* in the world, I considered the processual stages this required of the female person. I established womanhood as a phase in a female person's life where her productive and reproductive abilities become intertwined, which in turn served as a basis for her devaluation. As such, my supposition is that *Ìyá* as a category can be attained as one progresses in age and maturity as a female person. It can also be achieved by virtue of one's birth or marriage into royalty or economic affluent families, which can in turn influence one's political and economic status and subsequently though not necessarily, lead to a sociospiritual emancipation achieved through the cult of the mothers. It can also be an amalgam of these three factors. Our aim in this last section is to read some Yorùbá oral traditions along gendered lines.

Gendered Notions in Mythistories

Osun

Osun, as earlier explicated, is a primordial female deity (*òrìsà*), supposed to be the founder of the *Àjé* institution. In Yorùbá mythology, Òsun is said to have immortalized herself by becoming deified and is revered and traditionally worshipped at a designated shrine near the Osun River in Osogbo, Nigeria. Osun is described as the perpetually renewing source of life, as well as the appearance of sweet water from dry ground (Love 2012, 88).

In the Ifá literary corpus – the Yorùbá storehouse of wisdom – the *odu* Òseètúrá narrates how sixteen male deities sent to the world by Olódùmarè sidetracked Òsun. Following the inability of the male deities to bring things under control, they decided to go to Olódùmarè, who asked about their seventeenth person and why they did not consult with her:

> Won ni, *"Nitori pe o je obinrin laarin awon ni"* Olodumare ni,
> *"Agbedo o!*
> **Obinrin bi okunrin ni Osun"**

They replied,

> *"It was because she was only a female among them."* Olodumare said,
> *"May it not be so!*
> *Osun is a manly woman."*
> (Ogungbile 2000 in Olajubu 2003, 74; Oyewumi 2016, 46)[9]

Osun's femininity was clearly a sore point among the male òrìsà. She was considered *only a female* among them. More precisely, she was regarded as only a woman. The implication is that they were aware of not just the difference in biological sex but the more significant point that as female, Osun was not in their ranking. They were rebuked for their sexist reference by Olódùmarè (in the word "agbedo!"), who informs them that Osun is more than a mere woman: "she is a woman like a man."[10]

In what capacity can a woman be perceived to be like a man? In everyday rhetoric among the Yorùbá, such depiction is attributed to women who have performed daring acts (like Òsun) or heroic feats (like Móremí) or achieved economic and political exploits (like Efúnsetán Aníwúrà), acts that depict the strength of masculinity and transcend the softness and docility of femininity, with toughness being a prerequisite for maleness (Olajubu 2003, 23). Within the same rhetoric, what will a male who exhibits as docile be called? Womanly or woman like? This has often been taken as an insult, for it is seen as condescending for a man to act like a woman or be feminine.[11]

Moremi

In the narratives surrounding Moremi, we find a tale of bravery and sacrifice. Moremi, portrayed as a woman of great beauty, employed her charm in spying out the enemy's secret. Moremi sought the help of the Èṣìnmìrìn river and vowed to give whatever the river deity requested of her if her mission was successful. Moremi allowed herself to be captured by the enemy and became queen in the enemy's kingdom. This gave her insight into their military intelligence. Armed with information, she returned to her people in Ile-Ife and was able to defeat the enemy. The Èṣìnmìrìn river, however, demanded her only child as sacrifice for her victory. Moremi requested a reward from the King of Ife for her sacrifice. He pledged that descendants of Ife would continually be her children and hold an annual festival to immortalize and revere her.

Jacob Olupona reads the Moremi narrative as a "heroic identity [that] resembles that of the ideal man, the warrior hero" (2011, 208). He notes as well that one of Moremi's *oríkì* (praise name) deploys sexual imagery in describing her. She is described "as the heroine who conquered rebellion and overcame intrigue with her vagina (Morèmi a f'òbò ṣ'ẹ tẹ̀)" (ibid). This, Olupona suggests, raises the question of unequal power relations since the sexual imagery was employed by men to diminish Moremi's heroic act and accomplishment. In Olupona's account, we are brought face to face with the fundamental role that linguistic construction played in the portrayal of Moremi's heroic act:

> Morèmi's redemptive suffering is undertaken for the liberation of ifẹ̀, but her heroism is represented only by her sexual prowess and her conduct as a seducer – in the words of the myth, she is reduced to her "vagina." The

language used, which invokes female symbols and private body imagery, underscores the magnitude of her role in the salvation history of ilé-ifẹ̀ . . . it fails to accord her the glory that would be given to men who have achieved the liberation of their people.

(ibid, 209)

Moremi, a "woman like a man," is seemingly respected and immortalized and then belittled and devalued for the same heroic feats for which she is praised. This reveals the depth of sexism that exists among the Yorùbá.

Efúnsetán Aníwúrà

Efúnsetán Aníwúrà is recorded as the second *Iyalode* of Ibadan who reigned around 1871–1874. The title *Iyalode*, being a political one, is open to only the elite women of the state and is essentially a privileged position. Ibadan tradition holds the *Iyalode* as belonging to the inner conclave of the elder's council. Although a kingmaker, she is exclusively exempted from vying for the office of Olubadan. The different historical narratives of Efúnsetán Aníwúrà present rudimentary information about the rise and fall of a formidable female, one that could be described as "a woman like a man" because she embodied the masculinity of dominance. Efúnsetán was so powerful to the extent that her private army fought alongside the Ibadan army.

There is a certain degree of controversy surrounding the events that led to Efúnsetán's fall. Some accounts blame her fall on her refusal to support Latoosa, the commander in chief of the Ibadan military in his political ambition. Other accounts hold that the *Iyalode* at some point became a threat to Latoosa and his ambitions to ensure that his son Sanusi would succeed him. Latoosa unseated Efúnsetán supplanting her with her closest associate, "her Otun," who was coerced into assuming Efúnsetán's role. While intervening in what was suggested to be a household dispute, Latoosa facilitated Efúnsetán's death alongside torching her property. Some popular accounts, however, claim Efúnsetán was an oppressor and that her ruthless rule eventually led to her destruction.

Iyalode Efúnsetán Aníwúrà falls into my analysis of *ìyá* in the second category of female persons who wielded social, economic and political influence. She was, like Osun and Moremi, "a woman like a man." So, as *ìyá* she ought not be categorized as "a woman who exercised power and influence." These exalted female persons had broken the barriers that bound them to womanhood – the processual stage where female persons are derided, devalued and disparaged. As *ìyá*, they had crossed gendered boundaries and had become men. They presented a masculine personality through their heroic acts and socioeconomic cum political given. They were ontologically female persons, but socioculturally, they exhibited traits expected of men.

Another intriguing and pertinent theme regarding the Efúnsetán narrative found in literary works, such as Akinwunmi Ishola's – which consequently became the popular account – is the male-centric modification of the narrative. Efúnsetán's positive characteristics, such as her business acumen, her allegiance to her homeland and her ability to perform heroic acts in protecting and advancing Ibadan (Ogunleye 2004, 317), were downplayed at the expense of a male-centred view which instead venerated Latoosa, making the villain the victim. Foluke Ogunleye surmises that

> a preoccupation with a male-centric ideology motivated Akinwunmi Isola to demonize Efunsetan Aniwura in his play. Our historical analysis shows that Latosa was a more pronounced villain than Efunsetan ever was, yet he is portrayed almost as a saint and a crusader while Efunsetan is portrayed as satanic.... Isola's authorial interpretation of history is perceptibly tilted in favor of the male. He ... decries ... history to paint a bleak picture of the female.
>
> (ibid, 311–12)

The underlying moral suggestion for this is that society has encoded a male worldview to such an extent that it is assumed that women who rise to power often get intoxicated by it and as such become incontrollable. The implication by extension is not to make women humbler but to deter women from pursuing and assuming high-ranking positions and to give the men who work with such women the impression that they are 'less of a man.' The male-centric modification of canonical texts such as Akinwunmi's require re-reading and rewriting, a task I suggest should be in the precincts of an AFPL.

Gendered Notions in Ìjálá

Ìjálá, the hunters' chant in Yorùbá cultural performance, authenticates the exploits of hunters and warriors as heroic fearless acts. Bisi Ogunsina describes it as the Yorùbá hunter's verse that chants the praises of Ogun, the ferocious warrior, god of hunting, combat and all iron apparatuses (1996, 84). Ogunsina makes a further claim that "Ìjálá chants by women, about women, and from a female perspective, are rare" (1996). He attributes this to the mythical image of Ògún as one of domineering masculinity. This establishes a detail I have emphasized that women are not perceived in the Yorùbá oral traditions and society as brave and courageous, and the female persons who possess these qualities are considered women with manly abilities thus constructing maleness as the norm. Ogunsina further contends that "[n]either the artist, his language, nor his ideas are independent of his society, each of these affecting and being affected by the others" (1996, 83). The Ìjálá and its contents therefore

The Dehumanized Woman in History, Philosophy and Culture 67

reflect a patriarchal context that sidelines the capacities of the female persons. Some Ìjálá verses explicitly despise women:

Obìnrin l'òdàlè, obìnrin lèké
Obìnrin ò sé finú hàn

Women are traitors, women are deceitful
Women cannot be trusted to keep secrets
(Adegbindin 2016, 240)

As Omotade Adegbindin observes, "[s]uch identity is obviously an undue generalization about females and its truth questionable" (2016). He advances the importunate effect this has on society as having the tendency to exclude the females from holding prominent positions as well as creating a perception of the self that is limiting of the females, to the extent that it reduces the trust that ought to be placed on them.

A second slanderous and sexist Ìjálá chant goes thus:

Òbódìran
Òbó ò joyè
Òbó tó joyè
Ní bàlú jé
Ilésanmí l'obìnrin yíò má jé

The lineage of vaginas
Vaginas don't get crowned
The vagina that was crowned
Ruined the town
The private sphere (home) befits me is what a woman will be called
(Olademo 2010, 102)

This *Ìjálá* verse validates the public–private distinction that limits the active participation of women to the domestic sphere. It also considers women unsuitable candidates for political positions. The chant uses heavy sexual imagery that reduces women to their sexual organs. This reductive use of sexual imagery is also a common feature in some Yorùbá proverbs. Proverbs, a measure of a people's perceptive intelligence and cultural wisdom, constitute one of the cultural and patriarchal means for devaluing womanhood. These proverbs, alongside other aspects of the Yorùbá oral tradition which hold women in contempt, demonstrate how women's oppression is engrained in language, the ubiquitous channel through which women's oppression has been transmitted through the ages. This answers the question I initially raised regarding how patriarchy has been institutionalized and how it has come to reproduce itself: this has been done through language as used in sacrosanct oral traditions such as poetry like *ìjálá*, prose narrative like Efúnsetán Aníwúrà's, ritual procedures like Móremí's *Edi* festival and proverbs (*òwe*), as I will show in the next chapter.

Notes

1 See Ehrenberg, M. (1989). *Women in Prehistory*. Norman: University of Oklahoma Press. 77–81, 99–100, 103–107
2 A notable paradigmatic shift occurred in family structures alongside a near total blurring of the private and public spheres of home and work during the COVID-19 pandemic. The ensuing digital revolution made technology the way to go as all walks of life became digital by default.
3 Oyeronke Olajubu (2003, 90–91) provides us with a useful analysis of regency.
4 Kwasi Wiredu and Kwame Gyekye, for example.
5 See Kwasi Wiredu, Kwame Gyekye (1992), Olusegun Oladipo, John Ayotunde and Ishola Bewaji.
6 I use *becoming* and *being* in italics to denote a metaphysical essence rather than just a rhetorical function.
7 Italics mine for emphasis.
8 Note the tonal marks on *ìyà*, a term which translates as "suffering," and *ìyá*, which translates as "mother." This homonym is often used rhetorically to associate woman with the accompanying term suffering.
9 Italics mine for emphasis.
10 The interpretation "manly woman" by Ogungbile in my opinion downplays the force of the sexist notion in the statement. I have opted for a direct translation, which I italicized.
11 Love gives accounts of how some African American males perceived being a priest to a female Orisha like Osun as a challenge to their masculinity. See Love, V.E. (2012). *Divining the Self: A Study in Yoruba Myth and Human Consciousness*. Pennsylvania: Penn State University Press, pp. 94–95.

References

Adegbindin, O. 2016. *Gender Advocacy in Africa: Insights from Ifá Literary Corpus. Being and Becoming; Gender, Culture and Shifting Identity in Sub-Saharan Africa*. Ed. C. Ukpokolo. Camerron: Spears Media Press.
Afolayan, A. 2006. The Language Question in African Philosophy. In *Core Issues in African Philosophy*. Ed. O. Oladipo. Ibadan, Nigeria: Hope Publications.
Afolayan, A. 2017. *From the Cosmos to the Society: Worldview as/and Philosophy. Culture and Customs of the Yoruba*. Ed T. Falola & A. Akinyemi. Austin, Texas: Pan-African University Press.
Amadiume, I. 1987. *Male Daughters, Female Husbands*. London: Zed Books Ltd.

Bryson, V. 2005. Production and Reproduction. In *Marx and Other Four-Letter Words*. Eds G. Blakeley & V. Bryson. London: Pluto Press.
Dada, S.O. 2018. Aristotle and the Omoluabi Ethos: Ethical Implications for Public Morality in Nigeria. *Yoruba Studies Review.* Ed. T. Falola et al. 3(1).
Dahlberg, F. 1981. *Woman the Gatherer.* New Haven & London: Yale University Press.
Diop, C. 1989. *The Cultural Unity of Black Africa: The Domains of Patriarchy and of Matriarchy in Classical Antiquity.* London: Karnak House.
Du Toit, H.L. 2008. 'Old Wives' Tales and Philosophical Delusions: On 'The Problem of Women and African Philosophy'. *South African Journal of Philosophy,* 27(4).
Engels, F. 2010. *The Origins of the Family, Private Property and the State.* London: Penguin Books.
Farrar, T. 1997. The Queenmother, Matriarchy, and the Question of Female Political Authority in Precolonial West African Monarchy. *Journal of Black Studies,* 27(5):579–597. Sage Publications, Inc. https://www.jstor.org/stable/2784870
Gardner, C.V. 2009. *The A to Z of Feminist Philosophy.* Lanham & Plymouth: Scarecrow Press Inc. see entry on Patriarchy.
Gonzales, R. M. et al. 2017. The Bantu Matrilineal Belt: Reframing African Women's History. In *Gendering Knowledge in Africa and the African Diaspora: Contesting History and Power.* Eds. T. Falola, O. Yacob-Haliso. London & New York: Routledge.
Haslanger. 2000. *Feminism and Metaphysics: Unmasking Hidden Ontologies.* MIT.edu. http://www.mit.edu/~shaslang/papers/fmnewsUHO.html. Retrieved 26 March, 2020.
Ipadeola, A.P. 2023. *Feminist African Philosophy: Women and the Politics of Difference.* London & New York: Routledge.
Johnson, M.M. 1988. *Strong Mothers, Weak Wives: The Search for Gender Equality.* Berkeley: University of California Press. Accessed online 8 March 2020. http://ark.cdlib.org/ark:/13030/ft0k40038c/
Lawuyi, O.B. 2018. The Depersonalized as Vanishing Hero and Heroine. *Yoruba Studies Review.* Ed. T. Falola et al. 3(1).
Lerner, G. 1986. *The Creation of Patriarchy.* New York & Oxford: Oxford University Press.
Love, V.E. 2012. *Divining the Self: A Study in Yoruba Myth and Human Consciousness.* University Park, PA: Penn State University Press.
Macharia, K. 2012. How Does a Girl Grow into a Woman? Girlhood in Ngugi wa Thiong'o's the River Between. *Research in African Literatures.* Indiana University Press, 43(2).
McGee, K. 2015. The Impact of Matriarchal Traditions on the Advancement of Ashanti Women in Ghana. In *Listening to the Voices: Multi-ethnic Women in Education.* Ed. B. Taylor. San Francisco, CA: University of San Francisco.
Millet, K. 2000. *Sexual Politics: Manifesto for Revolution.* Urbana & Chicago: University of Illinois Press.
Molefe, M. 2020. *African Personhood and Applied Ethics.* Grahamstown, South Africa: African Humanities Program by NISC (Pty) Ltd.

Ocheni, S. & Nwankwo, B.C. 2012. Analysis of Colonialism and its Impact in Africa. *CS Canada Cross-Cultural Communication,* 8(3).
Ogunleye, F. 2004. A Male-Centric Modification of History: "Efunsetan Aniwura" Revisited. *History in Africa,* 31.
Ogunshina, B. 1996. Gender Ideology: Portrayal of Women in Yorùbá Ìjálá. *African Languages and Culture,* 9(1).
Olademo, O. 2010. Religion and Women's Sexuality in Africa: The Intersection of Power and Vulnerability. In *Women and New and African Religions.* Eds. L. Ashcraft-Eason, D.C. Martin & O. Olademo. Santa Barbara, CA: ABC-CLIO, LLC.
Oladipupo, S.L. 2018. Rethinking the Tripartite Conception of Person in Yoruba Traditional Thought. *Ewanlen. A Journal of Philosophical Inquiry.* https://www.academia.edu/40561458/3._Oladipupo_-_Rethinking_the_Tripartite_Conception_of_Person_in_Yoruba_Traditional_Thought. Accessed online 30 March 2020.
Olajubu, O. 2003. *Woman in the Yoruba Religious Sphere.* New York: State University of New York Press.
Olupona, J.K. 2011. *City of 201 Gods: Ilé-Ifè in Time, Space, and the Imagination.* Berkeley, California: University of California Press.
Oyeleye, O. 2018. Ìwà lewà: Towards a Yoruba Feminist Ethics. *Yoruba Studies Review.* Eds T. Falola et al. 3(1).
Oyeleye, O. 2020. Power Dynamics in Nuclear and Extended Families: A feminist Foucauldian Analysis. In *The Palgrave Handbook of African Social Ethics.* Eds. N. Wariboko & T. Falola. New York: Palgrave Macmillan, 29–30.
Oyewumi, O. 1997. *The Invention of Women: Making an African Sense of Gender Western Discourses.* Minneapolis: University of Minnesota Press.
Oyewumi, O. 2016. *What Gender is Motherhood: Changing Yorùbá Ideals of Power, Procreation, and Identity in the Age of Modernity.* New York: Palgrave Macmillan.
Oyowe, A. & Yurkivska, O. 2014. Can a Communitarian Concept of African Personhood be both Relational and Gender-Neutral? *South African Journal of Philosophy* vol. 33.1 pp 85–99.
Oyowe, OA. 2014. Fiction, Culture, and the Concept of a Person. *Research in African Literatures.* 45. 2:46–62 Indianapolis: Indiana University Press.
Paltasingh, T. & Lingam, L. 2014. 'Production' and 'Reproduction' in Feminism: Ideas, Perspectives and Concepts. *Sage Journals,* 3:1.
Parsons, T. & Bales, R. 1955. *Family, Socialization and Interaction Process.* Glencoe, IL: The Free Press.
Popoola, R.O. 2022. Gender Studies. In *Great Books Written by Africans across the Academic Disciplines.* Eds. Emmanuel D. Babatunde & Abdul Karim Bangura. Newcastle, UK: Cambridge Scholars Publishing.
Shehan, C. & Kaestle, C. 2009. Gendered Bodies in Family Studies: A Feminist Examination of Constructionist and Biosocial Perspectives on Families. In *Handbook of Feminist Family Studies.* Eds. S.A. Lloyd, A.L. Few, & K.R. Allen. Los Angeles/London: Sage Publications.
Trask, B.S. 2010. *Globalization and Families: Accelerated Systemic Social Change.* New York & London: Springer.

Wangila, M.N. 2010. African Women in Traditional Religions: Illustrations from Kenya. In *Women and New and African Religions*. Eds L. Ashcraft-Eason, D.C. Martin & O. Olademo. Santa Barbara, CA: ABC-CLIO, LLC.
Washington, T. N. 2005. *Our Mothers, Our Powers, Our Texts: Manifestations of Àjé in Africana Literature* Bloomington: Indiana University Press.
Wingo, A. 2006. Akan Philosophy of the Person. *Stanford Encyclopedia of Philosophy.* https://plato.stanford.edu/entries/akan-person/
Wiredu, K. 1992. The Moral Foundations of an African Culture. In *Person and Community Ghanian Philosophical Studies*. Eds. K. Wiredu & K. Gyekye, 1:104.
Wiredu, K. 2020. *Personhood in African Thought*. https://science.jrank.org/pages/7956/Personhood-in-African-Thought.html. Accessed online 7 April 2020.
Witt, C. 2005. Feminist Metaphysics. *Encyclopedia.com.* https://www.encyclopedia.com/humanities/encyclopedias-almanacs-transcripts-and-maps/feminist-metaphysics. Accessed online 26 March 2020.
Zeleza, T. 1993. Gendering African History. *Africa Development/Afrique et Développement.* Dakar: CODESRIA, 18(1): 99–117. https://www.jstor.org/stable/43658287

4 Between Proverbs and Postproverbials

In this chapter, I look at the nature of proverbs as a necessary rather than contingent attribute of language. I also consider the epistemic significance of proverbs in the entrenchment of patriarchal oppression. I excavate from the history of the Yorùbá language found in proverbs which derogates women and promotes inequalities. I employ the idea of postproverbials, which authenticate the presence of fresh proverbs minted from old ones and possessing new meanings and ideals. These new proverbs with new meanings and values, when appropriated for feminist purposes, are meant to facilitate the reconstruction of the traditional space of woman in ways that place the woman within a new rhetorical tradition that is egalitarian. Adapting these postproverbials to the fundamental task of recuperating the idea of woman is what generates the concept of feminist postproverbial as a methodological framework which laid the groundwork for an AFPL.

Proverbs as Performatives: A Linguistic and Philosophical Overview

Cultures are noticeably defined by language, and the element of language that captures a culture's values and beliefs at its finest are proverbs. Proverbs are used in literally every culture and language of the world. For most languages, there are undoubtedly several proverbs either collected and documented in major volumes or fossilized in the memory bank of the culture. In the culture and language of the Yorùbá, òwe is synonymous with the English proverb. Òwe is "a speech form that likens, or compares, one thing or situation to another, highlighting the essential similarities that the two shares" (Owomoyela 2005, 3).

Most definitions and conceptions of proverbs see them as simple, short, pithy, concrete, traditionally assumed truths, perceived to be commonsensical and derivable from experience. Proverbial truths, although derivable from experience, are often taken to be universal truths due to their rhetorical usage and currency within the culture. They are, however, in most cases, subjective truths. Barry Hallen (2000) makes this salient point regarding the assumed

Between Proverbs and Postproverbials   73

universality of proverbial truths in his claim that "proverbs do not introduce themselves to us as universal truths, as generalizations that always apply. Their pith, their point, their punch is situational or context-dependent to an essential degree" (2000, 141).

Another prominent and reinforcing feature of proverbs is that they encode a people's philosophy. For Yannis Tzifopoulos, "Proverbs are a form of wisdom (*sophia*) . . . they are remnants of ancient philosophy which was lost in major human disasters, and they are preserved because of their conciseness (*suntomia*) and dexterity (*dexiotes*)" (2013, online). Ademowo and Balogun define proverbs as exceedingly effective instruments for conveying cultural norms, worldview, values, etc. (2015, 10). F. I. Sotunde asserts that proverbs serve as beacons across the sociocultural terrain of human interactions and as such "are significant as an adjunct to philosophy" (2016, 3). Hallen caps this perception about the philosophical nature of proverbs with the claim that "proverbs have long been treated by anthropological and philosophical researchers as a legitimate source of African philosophy" (2000, 140).

Proverbs contain figurative language. Since it deviates from the conventional to convey deeper or complicated meanings, situating proverbs in context often makes it intelligible. However, a proverb can also suit different contexts. Hence, there is not one definitive context from which it derives its meanings. The context-dependent nature of proverbs constitutes a major constriction in assigning literal meanings to them. As Wolfgang Mieder notes, collected works on proverbs often catalogue proverbial texts outside of their social contexts; hence the use and purpose of these proverbs which are indeed context dependent are not revealed (2004, xii). However, Neal Norrick discusses the importance of fixity in forms and meanings of proverbs and thus considers literal meanings of proverbs, that is textual meanings, in understanding, interpreting and using them. Norrick notes that empirical studies have shown that the interpretations of proverbs crucially depend on their literal meaning. It is through these literal meanings that their supposed contextual meanings are derived (1985, 82). Norrick explicates further that "proverbs must be assigned literal readings before their figurative status can be assessed" (1985, 83).

Understanding that we can derive meanings from proverbs as texts – outside of extra-proverbial constraints – is quite reassuring. However, such an understanding of proverbs privileges their semiotic nature and leaves hanging their semantic function. Richard Honeck, from a linguistic standpoint, delineates proverbs as phonological, syntactic, semantic, pragmatic and semiotic entities (1997, 11). Among these five markers which form the linguistic structure of proverbs, the semantic and pragmatic aspects are of more importance and interest to the argument in this study.

Semantics refers to the analysis of the meaning of philological terms in a language outside of their contexts. It is equally the philosophical and linguistic analysis of meaning. It is preoccupied largely with the connections between words, sentences, signs and symbols and the signified – what they stand for in reality, their denotation. Peter Grzybek sees semantics in a narrow sense as the portrayal or explanation of the meanings of words as well as meaning change. In everyday rhetoric, however, it is used as a synonym for meaning. Grzybek (2014) defines proverb semantics as the meaning of a proverb and concludes that as such, "any attempt to explain or to interpret a proverb, i.e., to describe its meaning, could thus be classified as being semantic, and any description of proverb meaning would fall into the field of proverb semantics" (76).

Pragmatics, on the other hand, is basically the study of the *effect* of context on meaning. Pragmatics, as a theory of the science of language, has its roots in linguistics, psychology, anthropology, semiotics and the philosophy of language. Linguistic pragmatics looks beyond the literal or denotative meaning of linguistic expressions and considers how meaning is constructed while also focusing on implied meanings. Whereas semantics is interested in denotative meaning, pragmatics considers what people mean when they use language. According to Vida Jesenšek, "pragmatics commonly refers to the study of language use and theory of speech acts in concrete communicative situations" (Linke, A., Nussbaumer, M., & Portmann, P. R (1996) cited in Jesensek (2014: 144), 144). For Liam Magee,

> Linguistic pragmatics considers meaning a function of how words and phrases are used, famously coined in the Wittgensteinian expression "the meaning of a word is its use in the language." . . . Utterances can be understood as acts, and are best analysed in terms of their effects.
>
> (2011, 43)

Magee's analysis opens two fundamental areas which I will explore in order to engage these proverbs from both the linguistic and philosophical perspectives. These two areas are speech acts theory and Wittgenstein's conception of language as use.

In contrast to the theories of meaning that hold that linguistic expressions are meaningful because of the degree of their input to the sentence's truth conditions, speech acts explain linguistic meaning as an act in terms of the use of words and sentences. As a theory of meaning, speech takes its roots from the philosophical interpolations of the later Wittgenstein, Searle and Austin. Austin stressed the principal theme of Wittgenstein's later work, which is the idea that language is used for many and different purposes – and that simple, straightforward, literal assertion is only one of them (Blackburn 2020, 158). He classified speech acts into three kinds: locutionary, illocutionary and perlocutionary acts.

Locutionary acts, for Austin, are utterances, for example, to verbally abuse or defame a person entail using some words, and in articulating those words, the use of the vocal organs must be employed. Locutionary acts are therefore the spoken words or utterances a speaker makes and their literal meanings. Literal meaning here includes verbal and rhetorical meanings, which run correspondingly to the oral, syntactical and semantic aspects of any utterance that makes meaning (Pepe 2013, 522).

Illocutionary acts follow from the locutionary acts and rely on the pragmatic "illocutionary force" of the utterance (the locutionary act). According to Mitchell Green,

> an utterance . . . such as "You'll be more punctual in the future," may leave you wondering whether I am making a prediction or issuing a command or even a threat. The colloquial question, "What is the force of those words?" is often used to elicit an answer.
>
> (Green 2014, online)

Answering this question is like asking "what is done *by* or *in* the utterance?" Austin points out that perlocutionary acts relate to the producing *effects* because unless a certain effect is achieved, the illocutionary act will not have been successfully performed. Without an audience hearing what I say and taking it in a certain sense, I cannot claim to have warned them. For an illocutionary act to be carried out, an effect must be achieved on the audience (Austin 1962, 113–114). A very good example is the following: A speaker asks a hearer, "What is the time?" The locutionary act is the utterance, the illocutionary act performed is questioning and the perlocutionary act is the effect on the hearer, which more than likely will be the checking of a (wrist) watch so an answer can be supplied.

John Searle differentiates between indirect and direct speech acts. In the latter, the meaning is literal, not implied, while in the former, the utterer conveys more to the listener than she actually says as a result of their reliance on the background information that they commonly share. This for Searle can be "both linguistic and nonlinguistic, together with general powers of rationality and inference on the part of the hearer" (1975, 61). Consider the last example, for instance. Imagine that the request for time elicits the response, "half past seven" from the hearer. This is a direct speech act since it is a literal meaning. However, if the speaker in this context is the wife and the hearer the husband and they both have to ride in the same car for about forty minutes to get to work by eight o'clock, then the implied meaning could be that "It's seven thirty, and thanks to you we are late for work." Reversing the case, the speaker might be indirectly calling the hearer to notice that he was making them late for work, and rather than state this explicitly, the speaker can do so by asking what the time was to get the hearer to have a look at the clock and realize he is making them run late. Indirect speech acts do not have direct meanings; they contain what H. P. Grice calls *implicature*. This implies saying one thing and meaning another. It is in this sense of indirectness that proverbs operate as articulations and demonstrations of speech acts in specific communicative circumstances.

Proverbs, as earlier mentioned, are figurative. They depart from the literal use of words and as such can be said to be indirect speech. Owomoyela states that the root of *òwe* is in the verb *wé,* which translates as "wrap" and could also translate as "compare." *Owe* thus

> reveals an important Yorùbá view of what happens when one likens something to something else: one brings the two items into as close proximity as possible in order to make their qualities observable side by side or in (virtually) the same space; one intertwines them, in other words.
>
> (2005, 3)

Thus, *òwe,* like proverbs, makes use of indirect language while still making literal sense.

Norrick notes that proverbs, as speech acts, are inventoried. By this he means that, "[a] speaker who uses a proverb falls back on the traditional store of preformed utterances. Seen this way, utterances of proverbs are acts of quoting. But the speaker does not quote an individual author; he quotes the linguistic community itself" (1985, 26):

> Proverbs are therefore doubly indirect. First, they are quoted. As such they express observations not original with the speaker; the speaker need not take full responsibility for their form or content. Second, proverbs generate implicatures. The speaker means what he says on the literal level, but he means something more in context. It is up to the hearer to piece together the intended implicature.
>
> (ibid, 27)

Since implicature must be pieced together by the hearer, as Norrick suggests, proverbs become so dependent on context, and since contexts differ, so will their implicatures as well. As a result of this complication in deducing proverbial meanings, I consider the literal meanings of proverbs. Conversely, Mieder makes this observation that the implication and intention of proverbs are best unveiled through their use in actual communal situations (2004, 133). This observation intersects Wittgenstein's understanding of language as use.

Individual authors of proverbs are rarely known. What is known is that linguistic communities accept and use proverbs. The linguistic community serves as the repository for proverbs which are tacitly accepted by its speakers and hearers and taken in most cases as sacrosanct by the linguistic community. Considered as folk wisdom, proverbs are perceived to be the experience of many generations. For proverbs to thrive, they must be preserved by the linguistic community that produced or/and accepted them, and so do their meanings. This is because within linguistic communities, ideals and approaches regarding language use, variations and customs are a shared phenomenon (Morgan 2014, 1).

What I am calling the linguistic community, the later Wittgenstein conceives as life-form or form(s) of life. This refers to the cultural environment in which a language game occurs. Language games can be likened, in some respects, to an inside joke: you get the joke if you are in on the joke. Likewise, in language – and with proverbial expressions – you grasp the meaning if you are familiar with its usage within the context of the language. Wittgenstein goes on to give us what has become a maxim in the philosophy of language: "the meaning of a word is its use in the language" (1986, 43). The meaning as use theory in the philosophy of language is of key interest to our deliberations on proverbs. I work on the assumption that the meaning of "woman" will be found in its use in a linguistic community. I therefore ask again: how is woman used in (proverbial) language? However, before deliberating on feminist postproverbials which not only considers how "woman" is used in proverbs but aims ultimately to alter the linguistic conjuncture through alternative proverbial constructions, it is essential to consider 'postproverbiality' as a concept and ultimately as an indigenous methodology.

From Anti-proverbs to Postproverbials

Proverbial language in the West, prior to the advent of the mass media and new media, has continually witnessed alterations.[1] Anna T. Litovkina (2019) remarks that proverb alterations are not new and that they can be traced historically. Accordingly, she advances the unpopular belief (which I will return to subsequently) that "proverb alterations are as old as proverbs themselves" (2019, 28). Proverbial disruptions or proverb parodies are indeed innovative alternative reconstructions and reactions to traditional proverbs. These inventive reenactments of traditional proverbs have answered to a wide range of terminologies across various geographical and cultural sites, from anti-proverbs in the West[2] to postproverbials.

Anti-proverbs (*Antisprichwort*), a coinage of Wolfgang Mieder (2004), are alterations of customary proverbs essentially for the purpose of creating humour. Mieder defines the term as "parodied, twisted, or fractured proverbs that reveal humorous or satirical speech play with traditional proverbial wisdom" (2004, 28). A major feature of altered proverbials is that they retain some part of the original proverb, thus enabling the reader/hearer who is familiar with the original to perceive the violation or distortion that occurred between the old and the new. Litovkina, however, theorizes that some anti-proverbs have become so popular that they have in themselves become proverbials. For example, "A new broom sweeps clean, [but the old one knows the corners]."[3] Anti-proverbs, Mieder notes, are a clear indication that proverb form and phrasing are by no means sacred or inviolable (2019). The fixity of proverbs has indeed given way to fluidity. For Litovkina, while "the old proverbs acted as preconceived rules, the modern anti-proverbs are intended to activate us into overcoming the naive acceptance of traditional wisdom" (2019, 29).

A parallel concept to Mieder's anti-proverb is Aderemi Raji-Oyelade's postproverbials. Postproverbials are alternate fabrications imitative of traditional proverbs. These parodied proverbs oppose conventional proverbs and often make a jest of conventional and generally accepted proverbs. Raji-Oyelade defines postproverbials as "the synchronic imagination of alternate creations which accompany (side by side, almost functioning as parallels to) the utterance and use of conventional sayings" (2012, 41). Postproverbials are also radical speech acts. They possess both locutionary and illocutionary faculties as linguistic materials and cultural markers. Raji-Oyelade reasons that as speech acts, Yorùbá postproverbials (Yorùbá being the language in which they were originally conceived) have a huge inclination to limit their operations to rhetic acts.[4] Conventional Yorùbá proverbs contain both phatic and rhetic acts in their delivery. This determines their formulaic reference to being the elders' wisdom, and it thus warrants the accompanying introduction "awon agba wi" (*as the elders say*) prior to using a proverb, especially in the presence of the elderly. This, Raji-Oyelade asserts, is a clear example of a phatic, reported utterance. Since postproverbial utterances do away with this reference to the wits of the elders, they weaken the force of proverbs as oral forms of language transmitted with precision from generation to generation and conversely, the relative fixity of proverbs.

Much like Mieder's anti-proverbs, Raji-Oyelade's postproverbials reject fixed proverb forms. This comparative fixity or rigidity of proverbs, Raji-Oyelade attributes to the need to "transmit the verbal properties of the proverb, if not its conventional cultural meaning, with absolute consistency and fidelity to its original structure" (1999, 75). However, the postmodernist rhythm alongside its attending rhetorical tradition has necessitated a deconstruction of the margins of meaning that typify most traditional proverbs to suit postcolonial realities. The dissolution of this relative fixity of proverbs through deconstruction ultimately produces a postproverbial construction. It is in this sense that the postproverbial has received general approbation, especially from Wolfgang Mieder who notes that it fits "the specific African changes of existing proverbs more precisely" (2012, 15).

I earlier noted Litovkina's assertion that parodied proverbs are as old as proverbs themselves. However unpopular this claim might be, it opens up a new vista by which I can show postproverbials as parodied proverbs that are suggestively philosophical. My interest in the philosophical import of the postproverbials is not far-fetched. While this work leans heavily on the indigenous – the cultural and literary theory of the postproverbials – it is also deeply philosophical and unwaveringly feminist. Recognizing then that postproverbiality as an act had been performed by erstwhile philosophers was an interesting find. In the words of Litovkina, "Proverb alterations are as old as proverbs themselves ... in the eighteenth century the traditional wisdom of many proverbial gems was questioned by a number of philosophers, writers and poets ... who created and inspired many proverb transformations" (2019, 28).

Between Proverbs and Postproverbials 79

While I find Litovkina's pronouncement quite appealing, it is remarkable to note that there are interconnections between literary theory, through which the postproverbials gained much ground, and philosophy. "Among the connections between literary theory and philosophy are very strong affinities between deconstructive thought [à la Derrida] and the thought of the later Wittgenstein. The single most striking difference is that Wittgenstein does not take his deconstructions to have dramatic consequences outside philosophy" (Wheeler 1988, 239). Yet Wittgenstein's work has had tremendous influence outside philosophy, much as Derrida has influenced literary theory. Postproverbialism, as a cultural and literary theory, is a hybrid speech act which employs the method of deconstruction especially from its use in literary studies. Deconstruction in this sense differs slightly from its philosophical alternative, although it follows a similar fundamental strategy, which is to "follow the trace of a key ambiguity or blind spot through the text to illuminate hierarchical oppositions it relies on and the fault lines along which it can be undone" (Holland 2020, online). Darin Tenev captures deconstruction as "questioning the unquestioned presuppositions of every system under consideration, philosophical or otherwise" (2020, online). Deconstruction as the questioning of the unquestioned is simply what the postproverbial impulse has done within the context of the African proverbial parlance. The postproverbial agency turns conventional thought over its head. It is the tangible voicing of the deconstructive energies of the neo-competent speaker of the African language (Raji-Oyelade & Oyeleye 2020, 232).

For Raji-Oyelade and Oyeleye, "postproverbiality is purposively named and situated within a string of 'posts.' As such, postproverbials are postcolonial, poststructural, postmodern, linguistic reinventions" (2020, 232). It is in this sense that the postproverbials constitute a reflection of the postcolonial realities of African societies. This is not only because the explicit use of parodied proverbs became evident *post*colonial but also because its emergence in contemporary African society is, as Raji-Oyelade notes, indubitably "the effect of the interplay of orality and literacy-modernity, the critical correspondence between an older, puritanistic generation and a younger, disruptive, and somewhat banalistic generation" (Raji-Oyelade 1999, 75). Although this interplay of orality and literacy is often ascribed to the introduction of Western education in Africa, and the unfortunate consequence of self-alienating the Africans from their culture, the pertinent point for Afolayan is that "the 'memory-bank' model of language is not sufficient to sustain a post-colonial African culture. It has the sole disadvantage of stagnating the experience of the people and weakening their cultures' dynamism" (2020, online). Reacting to this need for dynamism in both language and culture positions the postproverbial within the poststructuralist school of thought.

Postproverbials, like poststructuralism, denote a modern challenge to traditional beliefs. As such, the postproverbials are poststructural since they do not only stand at variance with the norm but employ the Derridean concept of *différance*, a neologism which plays on the meanings of the words "differ" and "defer." For Derrida, différance suggests the many ways by which meaning is deferred. Postproverbials as such seek to create a difference not only in the ways these newly coined proverbs are rendered as different from the traditional ones from which it is derived but also how the meaning of proverbs, rather than subsist with a secure sense of meaning, can be deferred.

In *Philosophical Investigation*, Wittgenstein presents us with a momentous twist in what has come to be known as the rule-following paradox: "no course of action could be determined by a rule, because every course of action can be made out to accord with the rule" (1986, 201) as well as his solution to the paradox: "if everything can be made out to accord with the rule, then it can also be made out to conflict with it" (1986). Thus, in exhibiting our compliance with following the rule, we could by the same token exhibit a defiance, resistance, a disobedience or noncompliance to the rule. "What this shews is that there is a way of grasping a rule which is not an interpretation, but which is exhibited in what we call 'obeying the rule' and 'going against it' in actual cases" (Wittgenstein, 1986). While this statement by Wittgenstein is provocative, the theory has conceivably crafted "a solid groundwork for post structuralists to build on the idea that traditions can be altered, and a systemic destruction of traditional categories set in motion" (Oyeleye 2021, 56). Postproverbials likewise "go against" the norms, the structure and rules which had hitherto governed proverbs with their fixed and static features.

Like the idea of postmodernity, the postproverbial's use of playful parodies and pastiche seeks to produce a pristine from a passé. While pastiches are imitations of the style of another artist and have been used predominantly to imply the Other of high art (Hoesterey 2001, 1), parodies are imitations but with meditative embellishment for comic effect. While pastiches as the Other to an original celebrate, parodies are intended to mock the work they imitate. With pastiches and parodies as figures of intertextuality, and intertexuality itself being the common thread that links poststructuralism and postmodernism, the postproverbials become sturdily foregrounded as both poststructural and postmodern constructs. Raji-Oyelade's description of postproverbials as "playful blasphemies" plays on the postmodern understanding of the idea of "playful parodies." Contrary to the argument by some critics, like Iyabode Daniel, that referring to these new versions of proverbs as playful blasphemy devalues their ingenuity and innovativeness and that Raji-Oyelade's position is a rupture that downgrades the creative essence and usage of the new version of proverbs (Daniel 2016, 71), I restate the point that "playful parody" is essentially a postmodern style; the postproverbial then as a postmodern method is a playful parody. Postproverbiality becomes blasphemous because as a postcolonial construct, it takes for granted certain aspects of the once unquestionable (oral) tradition of pre-colonial Africa.

The postproverbial additionally serves as a theoretical lens through which methodical and logical enquiry and analyses occur. As a methodology, the postproverbial has been influential in the field of paremiology, which studies proverbs and proverbial constructions including within other academic disciplines. While it has gained grounds in such fields as literary studies and language studies, paremiology's engagement in feminist and gender studies is still quite embryonic. What is prominent within gender studies is an analysis and collection of sexist proverbs and postproverbials rather than a reconstruction of these sexist proverbial structures as postproverbials. Available literature has also yielded little in the grounding of postproverbialism as a philosophical concept. There has therefore been little reflection on how postproverbialism as a methodological framework could facilitate not only the rehabilitation of the concept of "woman" in African feminism but also become a method that can birth the emergence of an AFPL as the disciplinary platform for continuously engaging with the reconfiguration of the African woman's agential power following years of cultural and ideological subjection.

The Idea of Feminist Postproverbials

Feminist postproverbials are critical and reformative attempts to linguistically alter proverbial paradigms which are disparaging, denigrating and derogatory to woman. These proverbial paradigms are not only sexist and chauvinistic, they also critically place significant limitations on women's traditional capability to the point of generating inequalities founded on gender binaries. As a feminist standpoint, postproverbials call into question the cultural and ideological oppression of woman as expressed through the use of proverbial language. They therefore serve as the theoretical framework through which a new rhetorical tradition for woman is established. They also serve as the preliminary groundwork for the emergence of an AFPL.

Feminist postproverbials are analogous to conventional postproverbials in their shared postmodernity. However, unlike postproverbials, which are parodic and humoristic, feminist postproverbials, although they can be witty, are not constructed for humour. Feminist postproverbials are meant for the purpose of linguistic reinventions. Like the established postproverbial methodology grounded in poststructuralism, feminist postproverbiality also reacts to pre-existing structures that denigrate and dehumanize the woman. It is a response to tradition, a going against the norm. It is a critique of canonical beliefs about women, some of which appear as cultural constructs which implicitly or explicitly use sexual imageries and metaphors, transmitted through language, to *Other* the woman against the man. Being a poststructural notion, feminist postproverbiality is better able to comprehend, construe and alter the social environment by interrogating existing proverbial meanings that devalue woman.

Much as feminist postproverbials, like mainstream postproverbials, are postcolonial, poststructural and postmodern in approach, they are fundamentally oriented primarily towards the African feminist decolonialization project. Decolonization, as we noted earlier, is founded on the indigenous. It has been, following Spivak's analysis, about moving away from Eurocentric epistemologies which undermine indigenous epistemologies. Accordingly, postproverbials are significant aspects of indigenous epistemologies that possess the capacity for moving the decolonization project forward. Building on the indigenous, I argued earlier, calls for a critical engagement with both the colonial and indigenous knowledge systems as sites of knowledge production. Postproverbiality therefore finds itself in the crucial crevices between the internal and the external that are united in undermining feminine consciousness and subjectivity. Thus, following Spivak and Fanon, feminist postproverbialty becomes an act of epistemic violence that disobeys existing norms of conduct that have battered the psyche of the African woman for centuries. Feminist postproverbial, through the framework of an AFPL, is thus geared towards the cultural emancipation of the African woman.

In this regard, feminist postproverbial, as a framework for sociocultural change, is an attempt to infiltrate and subvert the basis of belief in the status quo, by transforming a time-honoured social order alongside its structures of power, the prevailing hierarchy in such binaries as man and woman and the customs and norms through which the ideological oppression of woman is cultivated and whose transmission occur primarily through the medium of language. As a subversive method, feminist postproverbialism seeks to forcefully infiltrate the traditional proverbial context through the deployment of counter-proverbial appellations that dislocate the old and encourage the reconstruction of demeaning patriarchal proverbs. In subverting the social institution of language both in its formal (written) and informal (spoken) forms, feminist postproverbials become a methodology that is immediately congruent with the works of feminist poststructuralists who opine that patriarchy and the hegemony that has enabled the intersectionality of the race/class/gender divide ought to be targets of some form of subversion.

For a postproverbial reconstruction to count as feminist, it must necessarily fulfil the feminist agenda of refuting and defying the putative patriarchal features which dominate literally every stratum of the social structure. While there have been many theorists who have worked within paremiology, as well as literary and cultural studies, on how women have been linguistically represented and oppressed through the use of proverbs, most of them have stopped short of proffering a pragmatic solution to circumventing this sociocultural situation. Irene Salami, in "Language and Gender," examines the works of some African playwrights, including herself, with a focus on how proverbs have been used to construct female identity. Salami argues that proverbs are not gender blind, and while she was unable to reconstruct these proverbs as a means of altering the existing state of affairs, she admonished that "[b]oth male and female writers . . . should engage in a radical dismantling of these male constructed proverbs, replacing them with proverbs that promote societal well-being and construct positive identities for women" (2005, 38).

Kamwendo and Kaya (2016), similarly catalogued a collection of southern and eastern African proverbs which entrench patriarchy. They contended that eradicating the prevailing gendered proverbs might be impossible, and as such, they aimed their study at "documenting and interrogating the gendered proverbs associated with both negative and positive connotations" (Kamwendo & Kaya, 2016, 92). Similar to Salami's suggestion, they recommend that gendered proverbs and related social practices ought to be recorded in order to advise policy makers and to also create awareness for the obliteration of these proverbs, thereby advancing the cause for gender parity. Considering Akan proverbs, Kamwendo and Kaya analyze the ways proverbs represent and institutionalize women's roles, position and identity in traditional Akan communities; they estimate that challenging proverbs is tantamount to sacrilege, so they equally advocate a "revolutionization of oral traditions to assist in the deinstitutionalization of the prevailing patriarchal discourses and culture in traditional Akan communities of Ghana" (2020, online).

Barasa and Opande attempt a sociolinguistic exploration of the proverbs of the Lubukusu and Ekegusii of Kenya, as well as their implications on gender identity and the achievement of the UN Millennium Development Goals. Their findings revealed that certain proverbs portrayed women "as inferior, worthless and weak" and then fit them into socially constructed and specific roles such as "domestic workers, wives and caretakers" (2017, 155). They conclude that women suffer linguistic disparagement as a result of their social positioning as the Other to man. They recommend eliminating or re-conceptualizing proverbs which bolster gender parity. They also agree on the need to reform language to suit the changing needs of the modern society.

While these essays might be considered fundamental as signalling some critical reflections on the situation of woman on the continent, they fail the methodological test of being philologically reconstructive or philosophically reformative of the ontological and sociological conditions of the African woman or even of facilitating the methodological transformation of African feminism. This is because while they did well in stating the problem, they did little in the way of redressing these oppressive proverbs through an imaginative reconstruction that has a philosophical and sociological agenda. There are, on the other hand, theorists who reconstruct oppressive proverbs which while they are not anti-feminist, are also not feminist per se. There are also theorists who reconstruct sexist proverbial language through the use of even more explicit sexist terms that further cement the denigration of the woman. In "Postproverbial Constructions and Selected Sex-Related Yoruba Proverbs and Proverbial Expressions," Ademowo and Balogun subject to a critical analysis fifteen randomly selected sex-related proverbial expressions alongside their proverbial reconstruction. The authors observed that other than for visual symbolism, the stating of genitalia in proverbs does not affect the actual meaning of proverbs, but with postproverbials, the situation differs because the named genitalia and sexual act become the spotlight (2015, 9). This observation, however, appears to be inappropriate in some instances. What appears to be the case rather is that some of the original proverbs considered by these scholars were implicitly sexist while their postproverbial variations were explicitly sexist. I give an example from their essay:

Original Proverb: Ope l'obinrin, gbogbo eni ba ni igba lowo nii gun (women are palm trees, anybody with ladder climbs them). (Anonymous)
Philosophical Meaning: Women are weaker vessels; like eggs, they are fragile.
Postproverbial: ope l'obinrin gbogbo enito ba ni condom lo n ba won sun.
Postproverbial Meaning: Women are ever ready for fucking, just get a condom and cajole.

To begin with, the literal definition given to the original proverb is incorrect. The word *igbà* does not translate as ladder. It is a climbing rope that serves as a means for climbing a tree especially by a palm wine tapper. Similarly, the philosophical meaning attributed to the proverb is also not appropriate. Palm trees are hardly ever characterized within the Yorùbá sociocultural milieu as fragile or weak and thus cannot be an appropriate metaphor for a woman as a weak vessel.

The saying better translates as, "Women are palm trees, whoever has the means climbs her." It is important that we take note of yet another word in the original proverb, the word *gùń*, which translates as "climb" but is also used to refer to the act of intercourse, for example with animals mating; it is also the root of the word *mágùń,* which literally translates as "don't climb." *Mágùń* is a charm used in entrapping wives suspected of promiscuity and in apprehending their lovers. The word *gùń* is thus used to implicitly denote just what the postproverbial version explicitly states as *ba sùn*, which is "to sleep with or engage in sexual intercourse with." The implication of this proverb in both its original and postproverbial form therefore is that women are accessible to anyone with the means. It intrinsically commodifies women. I will attempt a reconstruction of this proverb in the last section of this chapter.

In the "Proverbial Oppression of Women in Yoruba African Culture," Oladele Abiodun Balogun outlines a different linguistic understanding of gender that also speaks to the ways language codifies oppression. He argues that some Yorùbá proverbs which pertain to women contain elements of oppression and infringe upon the dignity and rights of women (2010, 21). His essay documents proof of women's oppression performed through proverbs in Yorùbá culture, underscoring their malicious effects as well as the struggle for gender equality (Balogun 2010). With the understanding that these oppressive proverbs require urgent and critical review, Balogun's essay supplies a deconstructive and reconstructive reading of some of these proverbs. While I question Balogun's reconstructive approach for not furthering the feminist agenda of defying patriarchy, I do advance its laudable reconstructive attempts.

Balogun raises three challenges that projects aimed at reconstructing oppressive proverbs might face: firstly, the possibility that proverb users would kick against it since proverbs are widely held as inviolable; secondly, the inclination that the process of reconstruction will be made needlessly complicated and thirdly, the likelihood that the importance of the project might not be easily understood and its impact laborious (2010, 34). The first challenge is perhaps the easiest to combat: resistance by the elders is only a matter of time as the traditional will eventually give way to the modern. To combat the second challenge, and despite lacking clear mechanics of reconstruction, it should be ensured that reconstructions are not complex. In combatting the third challenge, instituting a conscious change in the proverbial parlance, I suggest an unconsciously instituted change instead. This unconscious stage for instituting the change can be set through the utilization of both the traditional and the new media. Movies, novels, blogs, comedy skits, short videos and other elements that encompass popular culture surely have ways of transforming our minds and the society at large; therefore, engaging such media forms in instituting an unconscious change in the everyday rhetoric might be a good starting point.

Helen Yitah's "Fighting with Proverbs" emerges as a suitable prototype of proverbial reconstructions which fulfil the feminist agenda. Yitah examines how traditional Kasena women of northern Ghana with minimal or no literacy subverted and resisted a prejudiced oral tradition, an activity which an average Kasena person would rather not engage in since the culture considers proverbs the wisdom of the ancestors. The "proverbial revolt," as Yitah calls it, is similar to Raji-Oyelade's "playful blasphemy" because it is expressed in a playful way. According to Yitah, the women take advantage of the light-hearted relationship that exists between them and their husbands' siblings of the same generation to undermine and oppose sexist ideology found in their proverbs. Through this, they form a body of 'counter-proverbs' by which new meanings are established (2009, 74).

The major differences between the feminist postproverbial and Yitah's fighting with proverbs or proverbial revolt is that while the Kasena women who engage in this proverbial defiance have minimal or no formal education, the feminist postproverbial is perhaps a more academic exercise. Yitah's work on proverbial revolt is, however, yet another way of excavating doxa as popular opinion and as indigenous knowledge which has been incorporated as episteme/theoretical knowledge. Another discernible difference is that whereas feminist postproverbials are performed as deliberate acts of altering the status quo and as feminist intellectual obligations, the Kasena women achieved theirs only as a light-hearted but marginal attempt at deconstructing a solidly consolidated patriarchal social relation. As Yitah notes, within a playful, light-hearted conversation or relationship, it is possible to participate in an activity that would ordinarily have been regarded as disruptive. As such, this playfulness and light-heartedness becomes a suitable vehicle for these women to question the unquestionable and violate the inviolable nature of proverbs (Yitah 2009, 77).

Feminist Postproverbial Reconstructions

The critical prism of feminist postproverbiality as I earlier delineated offers a reformative platform for reconstructing proverbs which are sexist, misogynistic and derogatory to woman. This section is committed to reforming some of these proverbs. The methodology for reconstruction will simply be to state the original proverb, followed by a literal translation. This translation will then be subjected to a critical analysis of the epistemic significance of the proverb in the entrenchment of patriarchal oppression and the consequent sociological implications on African women. I will then suggest and justify possible feminist postproverbial reconstructions that can undermine the oppressive capacities of these proverbs.

It is important to state briefly that there are as yet no fixed guidelines for reconstructing postproverbials. Reconstructions can occur in either the initial clause or in the final clause and there can be many variations. This arbitrary nature of reconstructing postproverbials is a double-edged sword because postproverbials did not originally exist as academic exercises but rather a part of the postmodern imaginative rhythm of popular culture. Much like the new media has undermined the power of traditional media, leaving the creation of media content in the hands of anyone who dares to create and disseminate, the postproverbials undermined traditional proverbs, taking them right out of the hands and mouths of the elders who held them sacrosanct. As such, proverbs reside, regrettably, in the hands of anybody to alter at will.

Feminist postproverbial reconstructions, however, cannot enjoy the arbitrariness of their broader counterparts, largely because they are more academic exercises. This, perhaps, is my biggest challenge at this initial stage, a challenge which Balogun forestalled when he claimed that as an academic exercise, scholars may likely undercut the arbitrary nature of postproverbials and needlessly complicate the process of reconstructing them. Therefore, while the mechanics of reconstruction are still being developed because this work is still largely in progress, I will offer a few guidelines which I have adopted thus far. As I noted earlier, reconstructions can occur in either of the clauses of the original proverb. In some reconstructions however, the initial and final clauses of two proverbs can be merged as long as the outcome remains positive and suits the feminist agenda of subverting patriarchal structures. Let us make a noteworthy point here that feminist reformulations of negative proverbs are set not only to reconstruct but also to transform the rhetoric as much as possible from negative and sexist to positive and constructive speech. Lastly, the reconstructions are not set to respond in a tit-for-tat fashion, so I do not needlessly juxtapose woman for man in a bid to swap the negativity ascribed to the subject to the Other.

Proverb 1

FSH[5]: *the whip that lashes the senior wife, lashes the junior wife too.*
Woman: The whip that lashes the first wife must not be allowed to see the light of day (Yitah 2009, 80).

The Igbo version is rendered as
Utari a pia nwunye nke isi na eche nwunye nke abua n'azu uzo
(The cane used to lash the first wife is always at the back of the door waiting for the second wife)
Its Yorùbá rendition:
Ìpàṣán tí a fi na ìyálé ḿbẹ láàjà fún ìyàwó
(The whip used on the senior wife is resting on the rafters waiting for the new wife; Owomoyela 2005, 125)
Its East African (Kenyan, Bukusu) version:
Eyapa nabulobe elipa nabukelema
(The cane that beat the send away wife will also beat the incoming; Barasa & Opande 2017, 166)

The cogent point here is that some of these proverbs have variants across the continent.[6] The renditions of the proverb indicate the extent of control and power a man/husband exercises over the woman/wife. The proverb objectifies woman/wife as a body or entity to be whipped and kept in control by that act. Yitah (2009) makes a valid point in stating that the junior wife, who usually is believed to be the husband's beloved, is in this proverb consigned to the same status as the senior wife (2009, 80). As a woman and consequently a wife, regardless of being the favourite, one is subject to the same kind of containment. Yitah deconstructs the whip to contextually symbolize "any kind of compulsion that may be brought to bear on the wife to enforce compliance with her husband's (and his family's) wishes" (2009). This proverb outlines how the woman is caught up in a system of control and power tantamount to domestic violence even in relations with her husband, who then becomes all symbolic husbands. It further analyzes how this family system continues to ensure the reign of male dominance, even with the manifestations of female husbands. The postproverbial version that such a [whip of/for control] should not be allowed to see the light of day is quite apt. Mineke Schipper offers a Ugandan proverb that appropriately serves the function of a postproverbial rendition of the original proverb under consideration: "If a wife sees the stick that beats her co-wife, she throws it into the wilds" (1991, 34).

Proverb 2

Original proverb: Òpe l'obìinrin, gbogbo ení bá ní igbà ní gùń
(The palm tree, like a woman, is accessible to whoever has the means; women are like palm trees, they can be climbed by whoever has the rope)
Feminist Postproverbial (1): Òpe l'obìnrin, won fi gbo gbo ara s'ewa
(Women are like palm trees; they are beautiful all over)
Feminist Postproverbial (2): Òpe l'obìnrin, won ku ifarada
(Women, like palm trees, are very tolerant)

Reconstruction (1) likens women to palm trees, which are characterized as beautiful particularly because of their utility. The Yorùbá believe no piece or part of the palm tree is unusable: its fronds are used locally in the production of brooms, its trunk serves as a log which can bridge streams and oil is extracted from its kernel, which is also consumed as a snack. This utility is priced above the tree's physical looks. This cultural connection between beauty and utility is exemplified by the proverb *atare réni tún ìdí è se, ó ń fi òbùró sèsín; òbùró ì bá réni tún ìdí è se ìbá suwòn l'éwà ju atare lo* (the alligator pepper plant [as a result of its utility] is constantly weeded and pruned to make it more attractive than the òbùró [a red berry like plant]; if òbùró had received attentive care like the alligator pepper, it would have been more pleasant to behold). For the Yorùbá, the saying *iwà l'ewà* (character is beauty) associates good moral character with a person's beauty. Thus, we can associate the indispensableness of woman with the utility of the palm tree and appropriate it as beauty. In feminist postproverbial (FPP onwards) 2, women like palm trees are praised for their long-suffering and tolerance. The palm tree has a notable characteristic which is that it can weather the harshest of atmospheric conditions without twisting. The African woman is comparable to the palm tree in this regard as she is perceived as resilient and tolerant. This tolerance, I can convincingly argue, is borne out of the many years of enduring patriarchal oppression.

Proverb 3

Original proverb: Òbò ò ṣéé ṣe àlejò
(The vagina is not a thing for showing hospitality [Good things are not good for all purposes]; Owomoyela 2005, 131)
Feminist Postproverbial: aya eni ò ṣéé ṣe àlejò
(One's wife is not a thing for showing hospitality)

While this proverb connotes some form of positivity that one should jealously guard what one holds dear, its use of explicit sexual imagery objectifies the woman as a means of sexual pleasure, thus emphasizing woman's body and sexual allure over other attributes. Further, it constructs a sexualized identity of woman that commodifies her as an object lacking in dignity and self-esteem. A similar Gikuyu proverb places oxen alongside wives as non-charitable entities: "Wives and oxen have no friends (One cannot show kindness to the extent of giving away one's wife or one's ox.)" (Schipper 1991, 29). The feminist reconstruction retains the meaning of the original proverb and its implication by replacing the sexual metaphor and recuperating the woman as a respectable subject who cannot be toyed with. An Ashanti variant of this postproverbial reads: "A wife is not meat to be parcelled up and sent out to others (Ashanti, Ghana)" (ibid, 30).

Proverb 4

Original Proverb: Akesán lòpin Oyó; ilé ọkọ nibìsinmi obìnrin
(Just as Akẹsan is Oyọ's city limit, so a spouse's home is a woman's final destination; Owomoyela 2005, 440)
Feminist Postproverbial (1): Akesán lòpin Oyó; ilé eni nibìsinmi eni
(Akesán is Òyó's frontier, a person's home is her place of rest[7]
Feminist Postproverbial (2): Bí *Akesán tile jé òpin Oyó; Kò ní kí ilé okó jé òpin obìnrin.* (Even if Akesán is Oyo's frontier; the spouse's house (marriage) need not be a woman's zenith)

This figurative use of Akesán, an ancient boundary or frontier town of Ọ̀yọ́, is indicative of how matrimony is considered the zenith of a woman's achievement. The assumption that marriage constitutes a woman's greatest attainment continues to adversely impact and impair the aspirations of some women who unconsciously stultify their ambition by targeting marriage as the fulfilment of their womanhood. Being more academically superior, forward thinking or wealthier than one's husband is still frowned upon in some cultural quarters. Under intense pressure from patriarchal social forces, the woman is consequently moulded into a less authentic version of what and who she aspires to be. In existential terms, the woman lives perpetually in bad faith that ensures that she lives to satisfy societal and cultural imperatives while denying her own autonomously generated values and valuation.

Proverb 5

Original Proverb: Bí obìnrin ò bá gbé ilé tó méjì, kì í mọ èyí tó sàn
(If a woman has not lived in at least two homes, she never knows which is better; Owomoyela 2005, 111)
Igbo variant: Ogori luo di abuo, omara nke ka nma
(It is after a woman had married twice that she is in a position to know the better man)
Feminist Postproverbial: Bí obìnrin ò bá gbé ilé tó méjì, kì í ní ìrírí tó pò
(If a woman has not lived in at least two homes, she will not have much experience; Oyeleye 2021, 63)

Proverb 6

Original Proverb: Obìnrin so ìwà nu, ó ní òun ò lórí oko. When a woman is deficient in character, she blames her marital woes on ill-luck (Sotunde 2016, 384)
Feminist Postproverbial: Obìnrin so ìwà nu, ó se àwárí è ní rìn àjò
(A woman loses [her] character; she finds it in the course of her life journey; Oyeleye 2021, 63)

Proverbs 5 and 6, like proverb 4, are similarly woven around matrimony and the lot of "women." Both proverbs have both epistemic and moral significance. Barry Hallen rightly observes that "the epistemic criteria underlie and inform the ethical in an impressively systematic and coherent manner" (2000, 113). The word *mò* in the completing clause of proverb 5 translates as "to know." Epistemically speaking then, to know or tell a difference between two ends would require a knowledge of both. However, experiencing two matrimonial homes, as a woman, except in a case of spousal death, is frowned on, at least among the Yorùbá. In most cases, a woman moving out of her matrimonial home is seen as being intolerant or as having a character flaw, and this is what evokes the use of proverb 6. While the feminist reconstruction of proverb 5 takes an empirical stance in constructing knowledge even about existential issues on experience, the reconstruction in proverb 6 is established on the precept that what one loses can yet be found or regained. It indirectly alludes to experience garnered through the course of one's life.

Proverb 7

Original Proverb: Ìtàkùn ní ńṣe ikú pa òkéré; obìnrin ní ńṣe ikú pa ọkùnrin
(Vines are the death of squirrels; women are the death of men)
(As dangerous as vines are to the squirrels, so dangerous are women to men; Owomoyela 2005, 306)
Feminist Postproverbial: Ìtàkùn ní ńṣe ikú pa òkéré; oun tó wuníje ní ń pani
(Vines are the death of squirrels; a person's desire can cause their death)
(Or, As dangerous as vines are to squirrels, so dangerous can a person's desire be, if untamed)

Matricide and uxoricide can occur for so many reasons ranging from rage to mental disorder. Spousal death can also occur because of other reasons including natural causes and as a result of one's untamed desires. However, there is a cultural logic deriving from the low perception of women that holds wives responsible for whatever low point their husbands get to, even death. This is a rampant situation in Yorùbá society. Rather than hold the women responsible necessarily for the death of men, and thereby strengthen the culture of blaming wives for the death of their husbands, the feminist reconstruction puts an end to the blame game by attributing death to anyone's desires. This proverb wittingly, however, references a man's untamed appetites.

Proverb 8

Original proverb: Obìnrin bímo fún ni ko pé ko mo pani obìnrin ko bímo fúnni ko pe koma pani.
(Whether a woman has a child or not for her husband does not prevent her from killing him; Balogun 2010, 29)
Feminist Postproverbial: Obìnrin bímo fún ni ko pé ko mo lani, obìnrin ko bímo fúnni ko pe koma lani.
(Whether a woman has a child or not for her husband does not prevent her from prospering him)

This proverb, in Balogun's analysis, is purportedly used to admonish men (similar to proverb 7) that their deaths reside with/in their wives. In other words, the fact that a woman is able or not to procreate does not invalidate the possibility of the woman killing her husband. This proverb, like the previous one, therefore suggests that women cannot be trusted, however long they have been with their husbands; it overlooks the idea that men can similarly be the root cause of their women's death. Balogun offers this reconstruction:

Abimo fún ara eni kope ki a ma pa ara eni; a o bimo fun ara eni, kope ki a ma pa ara eni.

("Whether there is offspring between a couple or not does not prevent either of the parties persecuting the other"; 2010). While this reconstruction establishes the point of spousal murder despite the existence of children in the relationship or marriage, a feminist postproverbial does not seek only to reconstruct the proverb while retaining its original negative form. It seeks a transformation of the entire tone from a negative, sexist and misogynistic proverb to constructive, progressive and encouraging aphorism. The feminist reconstruction I proffer transforms *pani* ("to kill") into *lani* ("to prosper"). This feminist reconstruction thus parallels the saying that "there is a woman behind every successful man."

Proverb 9

Original Proverb: Fìlà lobìnrin, wọn kì í bá ọdẹ wọ ìtí
(Women are caps; they never accompany the hunter into the dense forest)
(Women do not stick around when their men suffer reverses; Owomoyela 2005, 305)
Feminist Postproverbial: Fìlà lobìnrin, wọn buyì kún orí ni
(Women are caps, they add value to the head; Oyeleye 2021, 66)

For Owomoyela, hunters probably do not go into the dense forest with caps on because the hunter's cap could be knocked off his head by branches. In the feminist reconstruction of this proverb, we reconstruct woman to be a person who adds worth, value, substance and beautification to the head as opposed to being a fair-weather friend. Women as caps also safeguard the head. This makes true the Gikiyu proverb that "The man may be the head of the home; the wife is the heart" (Schipper 1991, 29).[8]

Proverb 10

Original Proverb: Bí a bá ká okó mo obìnrin nídìí á ní kùkú ni
(If one catches a penis in a woman's vagina, she will argue that it is only a corncob)
(Trust a woman to deny even the obvious; Owomoyela 2005, 242)
Feminist Postproverbial: Bí a bá ká ñkan mo obìnrin nídìí; bi o sowo, a somo
(If one catches something underneath a woman, if it isn't money then it is a child)

The reconstruction here portrays women as astute, prudent and discreet in their financial dealings. The word *ìdí* in *nídìí*, apart from its reference to the vagina, also translates as "underneath" or underbelly. Rather than employ it in the same sense as it was used in the original proverb, the reconstruction employs the term in another sense to reference the financial acumen of the woman. As part of their toilette, traditional Yorùbá women wore undergarments that had a secret pouch in which they could keep money. This shrewdness in financial dealings is what the feminist reconstruction compliments and commends women for. Similarly, the postproverbial extols a woman's/ mother's role in childbearing and rearing. Woman's prudence, both in financial matters and in child nurturing, is upheld by the feminist postproverbial version of the proverb.

Proverb 11

For proverb 11, I use an instance advanced by Yitah.
Proverbs:
Once you sleep with the chief's wife, you might as well continue until she bears your child.
A woman who kills a python must not go on to cut off its head.
Counter-proverb:
If neither cutting off the snake's head nor leaving it on will bring you peace, then crush it (Yitah 2006, 245).

Proverb 12

Original Proverb: A mother of only daughters does not laugh before the others (Rwanda)
She is less respected than the mother of sons (Schipper 1991, 43).
Feminist Postproverbial: A mother of only daughters laughs longest.

This feminist reconstruction, similar to Yitah's prior example, employs two existing proverbs in one feat. Rather than becoming less respected, this reconstruction suggests that she triumphs. This reconstruction is implicitly tied to a popular belief among the Yorùbá that female children are more caring towards parents especially as the parents age and become less able to physically care and maintain their independence. The reconstruction is thus a combination of the initial clause in the original proverb and the completing clause of the proverb, "S/he who laughs last, laughs longest (or best).

Proverb 13

Original Proverb: (a) Woman is like the earth: everyone sits down on her (Lingala, Zaïre)
(b) Woman is like the earth: even a fool sits down on her (Lulua, Zaïre) (Schipper 1991, 24)
Feminist Postproverbial: Woman is like the earth: everyone receives nourishment from her.

In this twelfth proverb, a woman is likened to the earth (ground), subject to all forms of defilement. The femininization of nature and the naturalization of women – the idea that women and nature are innately linked – has indeed been an implicit acknowledgement of their mutual exploitation. Women's implied association with nature has simply made it easier to entrench their domination and subordination in the same way as nature has been exploited and subordinated. Carolyn Merchant, in *The Death of Nature*, investigates the sexist assumptions inherent in nature as the benevolent mother and the patriarchal contexts in which the subordination of the earth, through scientific revolution and industrialization, occurred. The earth, as land, is also in economic terms, the first factor of production providing income and nourishment to plants, humans and animals alike. It is in this latter sense that the feminist postproverbial version considers woman to be like the earth, a source of sustenance and nourishment to all.

Proverb 14

Original Proverb: A woman with withered breasts drinks beer like a man (Ganda, Uganda)

After menopause, women arrogate certain rights (Schipper 1991, 49)
Feminist Postproverbial: A daring woman drinks beer even better than a man.

Naturally, breast ptosis occurs as women age. Attaching this change in breast appearance to a woman's ability to drink beer is sexist. I previously asked, "In what regard or capacity can a woman be described to be like a man?" I answered that among the Yorùbá, manly attributes are ascribed to women perceived to have performed daring acts (like Òsun), heroic feats (like Móremí) or economic and political exploits (like Efúnsetán Aníwúrà). Such acts obviously transcend the softness and docility expected of femininity in contrast with the strength of masculinity. This understanding indeed necessitated the feminist reconstruction I gave. It is also important to note that the alteration in the proverb did not occur in the completing clause as in most postproverbial reconstructions. Alterations can occur in any part of the proverb, and in this instance, the alteration happened in the initial clause. The reconstruction alludes to the saying, "what a man can do, a woman can do even better."

Proverb 15

Original Proverb: A woman is like the merino sheep: her beauty is judged by her backside (Sotho, South Africa/Lesotho) (Schipper 1991, 55)
Feminist Postproverbial: If a woman is like a merino sheep, her beauty would be judged by her economic power.

Proverb 16

Original Proverb: Love for a girl lies below the navel (Rwanda, Rwanda) "One likes things for their utility. The utility of a woman is to bear children" (Schipper 1991, 59).
Feminist Postproverbial: Lust for a woman lies below the navel; love for a girl lies deep in the heart.

Like proverb 2, proverbs 15 and 16 institute the utility of woman as a sex object. Proverb 15 reduces a woman's beauty to the woman's buttocks. The reconstruction, however, considers the economic value attached to the merino sheep and suggests this economic value as what a woman shares with the merino sheep. The feminist reconstruction for proverb 16 takes the focus away from the nether regions for a girl and instead rests the attention on the magnitude or depth of love which should be offered to her. The reconstruction in proverb 16 draws a distinction as well between a woman and a girl, suggesting that if at all a woman is sexually objectified, a girl should be endeared.

Proverb 17

Original Proverb: A very beautiful woman is either a witch or a prostitute (Sara, Chad) (Schipper 1991, 57)
Feminist Postproverbial: A very beautiful woman is pleasant to behold.

Proverb 18

Original Proverb: The kind woman has a hairless vagina (Mamprusi, Burkina Faso)
"For a woman to have abundant hair on her private parts is a sign of health and fertility.
Kind people are not wealthy" (Schipper 1991, 62).
Feminist Postproverbial: A kind woman (despite her kindness) is not afraid of setting limits.

Proverbs 17 and 18 both query a woman's virtue. According to the former, a beautiful woman is more than likely a witch or a prostitute. A Yorùbá proverb has a similar connotation: *eni bi arewa, bi iyonu* ("whoever births a beautiful girl, births trouble"). These proverbs indicate that being beautiful is itself a problem. Another Yorùbá proverb holds that *oju kii ri arewa ko ma ki*, meaning, "the eye cannot behold a beautiful woman without appreciating/acknowledging her." It is this latter proverb that influences the feminist reconstruction of proverb 17. Proverb 18 on the other hand is covertly sexist. Associating a woman's kindness to a hairless vagina is akin to saying that the woman's kindness is her inability to refuse sexual advances and thus the reason for her hairless vagina. The reconstruction suggests that a woman's kindness should not be taken for granted and must not be seen as a reason to take advantage of her. Being kind does not mean one cannot set limits on one's willingness to give.

Proverb 19

Original Proverb: To marry a woman is to marry palavers (Kongo, Zaïre) (Schipper 1991, 76)
Feminist Postproverbial: Marriage is not a bed of roses.

As exemplified in this feminist postproverbial, some reconstructions can simply be a saying or yet another proverb used as a counter saying. Palavers in marriages cannot simply be the fault of the woman or viewed only from a woman's perspective. They are intrinsic to most marriages, and the reconstruction simply factors this point into the new postproverbial.

Proverb 20

Original Proverb: Woman is the source of all evil; only our soul saves us from the
harm she does (Schipper 1991, 83).
Feminist Postproverbial: The human mind is the source of all evil; may our soul save us from the harm it conceives.

Mineke Schipper's (1991) book *Source of All Evil* takes its title from this last proverb. Arguing about the authority, users and perspectives of certain proverbs, Schipper contends that "the majority of proverbs seem to underline the authority of the quotes and implicitly of their users, whose perspective can sometimes be identified as male" (5). She gives the example of proverb 20 as one that cannot be logically used by women and could not have taken its origin from women's perspective. The reconstruction ascribes evil to the human, rather than woman's, mind.

To conclude this chapter, let us consider this statement by Schipper:

> I have often asked African friends interested in proverbs on women whether they knew of similar negative proverbs used by women about men. They were unable to think of any, nor was I able to find any convincing example of such proverbs in the African collections I read.
>
> (Schipper 1991, 12)

Schipper attributes this seeming lack of negative proverbs about men by women to the unequal relationship that exists between men and women in the region under consideration. According to her,

> In all unequal human relationships, the masters allow themselves to speak freely and openly about their subordinates. Being in power, they can afford to do so without any risk. Slaves, serfs, servants, colonized and other subjects, however, keep their thoughts and comments on their superiors to themselves, since they are scared of the repercussions such boldness might provoke.... Colonial Europeans, for example, generally did not know at all what Africans thought of them, communication on an equal footing being impossible in colonial relations.
>
> (Schipper 1991, 12)

Patriarchy, as earlier elaborated upon, parallels a colonial relationship. In such a power matrix, language is essentially controlled by the master; in the African proverbial context, the authority, use and perspective of most of the proverbs is male and biased. Pondering on what will become of these "horses of speech"? Schipper suggests that "it might be interesting to replace in proverbs the negative by the positive, the word woman/female by the word man/male and vice versa, not as a solution but as an exercise, to see what it looks like from the other side" (1991, 16). Schipper gives us a strong reason for this:

> Given the changes among women and societies, a number of proverbs no longer reflect certain women's realities today, particularly in the urban areas. Still, many proverbs in many cultures continue to represent deep-rooted ideas on women's roles and (im)possibilities. Where the proverbs are no longer quoted, these ideas do not seem to disappear naturally at the same time. Internalized images, collective memories and traditions are handed down from one generation to the next and are fundamental to the construction of people's everyday realities . . .
>
> (1991, 5–6).

Further, Schipper purports that, "[W]here old proverbs lose their relevance, they will be forgotten, but wherever the need for new ones is strongly felt, they will certainly be created. As the Ganda put it: 'An old proverb authorizes a new one'" (1991, 16). A major objective of this work is not just to create new proverbs from the old or to simply replace the negative with the positive. Beyond the exercise of feminist reconstructions, I aspire to open a new discursive space in African feminist scholarship that can serve as reference point for engaging with language as an essential and enduring stimulus for social change. This, I argue, is the justification for an AFPL.

Notes

1 Proverbial alteration in Africa thus far appears to be a postcolonial trend; hence I specify here that it is not new to the West.
2 This is a generalization accepted in the field of paremiology. See Mieder (2003, 2004), Litovkina (2019) and Mieder and Litovkina (1999). Germans typically might use *verballhornte Parömien*, while the French might use *perverbe* or faux proverb.
3 The twist in this proverb is an add on which I have in brackets.
4 Rhetic acts belong to J.L. Austin's three basic axes of locutionary acts, the other two being phonetic and phatic acts.
5 FSH according to Yitah is an abbreviation/acronym for Female symbolic husband
6 Mineke Schipper also notes that there are variants of this same proverb in Mamprusi, Burkina Faso and Krio, Sierra Leone (1991, 33).
7 This reconstruction can also be found in Oyeleye, O. (2020). Language Game and the Inequality of Gender. In *Identities, Histories and Values in Postcolonial Nigeria.* Ed. A. Afolayan. London: Rowman and Littlefield.
8 This reconstruction and the subsequent proverb might be seen as reinforcing a patriarchal assumption about the man being the head of the home. However, it, situates woman as equally important to the home rather than the fickle and untrusty ascription which the original proverb upholds.

References

Ademowo, A.J. & Balogun, N.O. 2015. Proverbial Constructions and Selected Sex- Related Yoruba Proverbs and Proverbial Expressions. *Antropologija*, 15(2).

Afolayan S. The Question of a Post-Colonial Culture: Language. *Ideology and Cultural Essentialism*. Retrieved online 6 July, 2020. https://legacy.chass.ncsu.edu/jouvert/v7is1/afola.htm

Austin, J.L. 1962. *How to do Things with Words*. Eds. J.O. Urmson & M. Sbisa. Oxford: Clarendon Press.

Balogun, O.A. 2010. Proverbial Oppression of Women in Yoruba African Culture: A Philosophical Overview. *Thought and Practice: A Journal of the Philosophical Association of Kenya* (PAK) New Series, 2(1).

Barasa, M.N. & Opande, I.N. 2017. Proverbs in Lubukusu and Ekegusii in Kenya: Empowering or Disempowering for Women and Girls? *Africology: The Journal of Pan African Studies*, 10(7).

Blackburn, S.W. 2020. Philosophy of Language. *Encyclopedia Britannica*. https://www.britannica.com/topic/philosophy-of-language/Practical-and-expressive-language#ref924158. Accessed online 3 June 2020.

Daniel, I.O.A. 2016. Proverbs and Modernity: Taking the Proverbs out of the Mouth of the Elderly. *Proverbium*, 33:71.

Green, M. 2014. Speech Acts. *Stanford Encyclopedia of Philosophy*. https://plato.stanford.edu/entries/speech-acts/

Grzybek, P. 2014. Semiotic and Semantic Aspects of the Proverb. In *Introduction to Paremiology: A Comprehensive Guide to Proverb Studies*. Eds. H. Hrisztova-Gotthardt & M.A. Varga. Warsaw & Berlin: De Gruyter Open Ltd.

Hallen, B. 2000. *The Good, The Bad and The Beautiful: Discourse About Values in Yoruba Culture*. Bloomington & Indianapolis: Indiana University Press.

Hoesterey, I. 2001. *Pastiche: Cultural Memory in Art, Film, Literature*. Bloomington: Indiana University Press.

Holland, N.J. 2020. Deconstruction. *Internet Encyclopedia of Philosophy* https://www.iep.utm.edu/deconst/. Accessed online 28 June 2020.

Jesensek, V. 2014. Pragmatic and Stylistic Aspects of Proverbs. *Introduction to Paremiology: A Comprehensive Guide to Proverb Studies*. Eds. H. Hrisztova-Gotthardt & M. A Varga. Warsaw & Berlin: De Gruyter Open Ltd.

Kamwendo, J. & Kaya, H.O. 2016. Gender and African Proverbs. *Studies of Tribes and Tribals*, 14(2).

Linke, N. & Portmann, 1996 cited in Jesenšek, V. 2014. Pragmatic and Stylistic Aspects of Proverbs. In *Introduction to Paremiology: A Comprehensive Guide to Proverb Studies*. Eds. H. Hrisztova-Gotthardt & M.A. Varga. Warsaw & Berlin: De Gruyter Open Ltd.

Litovkina, A.T. 2019. *Women Through Anti-Proverbs*. Cham, Switzerland: Palgrave Macmillan.

Magee, L. 2011. The Meaning of Meaning: Alternative Disciplinary Perspectives. In *Towards a Semantic Web: Connecting Knowledge in Academic Research*. Eds. B. Cope, M. Kalantzis & L. Magee. Oxford: Chandos Publishing.

Mieder, W. 2004. *Proverbs: A Handbook*. Westport, CT & London, UK: Greenwood Press.
Mieder, W. 2012. *Foreword in Playful Blasphemies: Postproverbials as Archetypes of Modernity in Yoruba Culture*. Trier: Wissenchaftlicher Verlag.
Morgan, M.H. 2014. *Speech Communities*. Cambridge: Cambridge University Press.
Norrick, N.R. 1985. *How Proverbs Mean: Semantic Studies in English Proverbs*. Berlin, New York & Amsterdam: Mouton Publishers.
Owomoyela, O. 2005. *Yorùbá Proverbs*. Lincoln & London: University of Nebraska Press.
Oyeleye, O. 2021. The Language Game and the Inequality of Gender: Interrogating Feminist Postproverbials. In *Identities, Histories and Values in Postcolonial Nigeria*. Ed. A. Afolayan. London: Rowman and Littlefield.
Pepe, C. 2013. *The Genres of Rhetorical Speeches in Greek and Roman Antiquity*. Leiden & Boston: Brill.
Raji-Oyelade, A. 1999. PostProverbials in Yoruba Culture: A Playful Blasphemy. *Research in African Literatures*, 30(1). Indiana University Press.
Raji-Oyelade, A. 2012. *Playful Blasphemies: Postproverbials as Archetypes of Modernity in Yoruba Culture*. LuKA Series.
Raji-Oyelade, A. & Oyeleye, O. 2020. The Postproverbial Agency: Texts, Media and Mediation in African Cultures. *Matatu: Journal for African Culture and Society*, 51(2). Brill Rodopi.
Salami, I. 2005. Language and Gender: A Feminist Critique of the Use of Proverbs in Selected African Dramatic Texts. *Ufahamu: A Journal of African Studies*, 31:1–2.
Schipper, M. 1991. *Source of All Evil: African Proverbs and Sayings on Women*. London & Kent: Allison and Busby Books.
Searle, J. 1975. Indirect Speech Acts. In *Syntax and Semantics 3: Speech Acts*. Eds. P. Cole & J. Morgan. New York: Academic Press.
Sotunde, F.I. 2016. *Yorùbá Proverbs and Philosophy*. Abeokuta, Nigeria: F.I. Sotunde.
Tenev, D. 2020. Jacques Derrida. Oxfordbibliographies.com https://www.oxfordbibliographies.com/view/document/obo-9780190221911/obo-9780190221911-0003.xml. Accessed online 28 June 2020.
Tzifopoulos, Y. 2013. Proverbs, greek. In *The Encyclopedia of Ancient History*. First edition. Eds. R.S. Bagnall, K. Brodersen, C.B. Champion, A. Erskine & S.R. Huebner. Blackwell Publishing Ltd. DOI: 10.1002/9781444338386
Wheeler III, S.C. 1988. Wittgenstein as Conservative Deconstructor. *New Literary History*, 19(2).
Wittgenstein, L. 1986. *Philosophical Investigations*. Trans. G.E.M. Anscombe. Oxford, UK: Basil Blackwell.
Yitah, H. 2006. Throwing Stones in Jest: Kasena Women's "Proverbial" Revolt. *Oral Tradition*, 21(2).
Yitah, H. 2009. "Fighting with Proverbs": Kasena Women's (Redefinition of Female Personhood through Proverbial Jesting. *Research in African Literatures*, 40(3).

5 Towards an African Feminist Philosophy of Language

Beyond the exercise of feminist proverbial reconstructions which I perceive to be a part of the solution to minimizing the sexual asymmetry expressed through the medium of proverbial language, I expect that this exercise will eventually instigate the opening of a new discursive space in African feminist scholarship that will consolidate what I identify as an African feminist philosophy of language. This chapter attempts a preliminary outline of the conditions necessary for the emergence of such a discursive space. African feminist philosophers should take language as a fundamental decolonizing space that can help in furthering not only the intellectual responsibilities of African feminists and feminist philosophers, but also help in pushing the agenda of social change.

Language as a Feminist Problem in the Western Sense

Feminist philosophers of language alongside feminist language reformers have argued that language, particularly the English language, is masculine in character (Penelope 1990; Spender 1990). Opposing the widely held assumption that language is gender neutral, feminist philosophers have argued that language and language use are not only gendered but also androcentric. The generic use of "man" and "he" to refer to the human species, as opposed to the specific use of "woman" and "she," is a clear demonstration of this bias. Saul and Diaz-Leon (2018) dubbed this the "Maleness of Language" and argued that English language is male in a similar way to how some expressions can be considered male. That such expressions encode a male worldview simply means that people grow up indoctrinated into the male order of things, which language helps to transmit. Encoding maleness keeps women on the sidelines and institutes maleness as a standard thus helping to subordinate women or to render them invisible.

In Protagoras' popular dictum, "Man is the measure of all things," 'man' appears to have been used in a generic sense. However, when "woman" is used interchangeably in the statement, it becomes "woman is the measure of all things." With this, the meaning of the maxim becomes confusing. Woman

DOI: 10.4324/9781032706382-6

is not generic, woman is specific while man, depending on the usage, can be both specific and generic. Similarly, the male pronoun "he" is also used in some generic sense.

This supposedly false gender neutrality has come under attack by some feminists (Moulton 1981a; Mercier 1995; Bodine 1998), who posit that these terms, in as much as they are intended to generate an idea of gender neutrality, do not essentially do so. Saul and Diaz-Leon (2018) posited that ascribing the terms "man" and "he" as gender neutral are indeed classificatory errors. They suggest that more careful work is done with respect to the meanings of these words. They submit that gender neutrality is way more complex than it appears to be. DuBois et al. (1987) suggest that the use of these supposed gender neuters are no mere grammatical conventions. The uses of "he" and "man" "can set up a context of expectation that, however unintentionally, excludes women from consideration" (1987, 106). For example, a statement such as "The last person to leave the room should ensure *he* switches off the lights" can suggest that there are no females among them.

Invariably, feminists have argued that the generic use of such terms has simply made women invisible. In line with Bodine's (1998) suggestion, the increasing opposition to sex-based hierarchy has resulted in noticeable change in the structure of English third person pronouns. Thus, the use of "they," for instance, has become more nuanced and inclusive of both sexes in ways that generate new social practice. Feminists' objections to the use of these gender neuters have considerably increased the visibility of women.

Feminist philosophers of language have also raised objections against the use of gender-specific occupational terms like "lady doctor," "waitress" and "proprietress." While these draw attention to the sex of the job holder as female and hence would not count as contributory to women's inconspicuousness, these terms are found questionable by feminist theorists who intend to reform language. The simple reason for this, Saul and Diaz-Leon note, is because it appears to be founded on the notion that maleness is a standard, as such women who take on these roles are somehow abnormal (2018, online).

To understand this better, I consider occupational terms with the suffix "man" such as policeman, salesman, fireman, chairman, postman and milkman, which were traditionally perceived to be male domains but now have women flourishing in them and as such require gender-neutral terminologies. The central argument for maleness as a norm can be summarized following Moulton's analogy of labels like Hoover and Scotch tape, which became the standard names for their product types. For Moulton (1981a), the carrying on with these job names like they were free of gender-bias is a figurative way of insulting women. Reforms in this respect have been numerous and the changes accepted by society. Therefore, terms like police officer, salesperson, fire fighter, chairperson and post person, have become accepted. Why there is no gender-neutral word for milkman seems hinged on the idea that it is no longer a sustainable career. Although lawyers, surgeons, teachers and engineers retain their original terms, it has been suggested that the image formed at the back of our minds about the sex of the job holder is often gendered.[1] Until recently, surgeons and engineers were not envisioned as female occupations. Such gender markings in job titles have in some ways codified a male worldview.

Susan Ehrlich and Ruth King proposed a similar idea in their claim that "[T]he 'names' that language attaches to events and activities, for example, those related to sex and sexuality, often encode a male perspective" (1998, 165). Saul and Diaz-Leon (2018) take terms such as foreplay and sex to be gendered female and male accordingly with sex being delineated in relation to male orgasm and foreplay in terms of feminine orgasm. Ehrlich and King discuss Cameron's views on examples such as *"penetration, fuck, screw, lay*, all of which turn heterosexual sex into something men do to women" (1998, 165). Similarly, they portend that "the absence of 'names' representing women's perceptions and experiences also reveals a male bias" (1998, 165). The term "sexual harassment," for example, Saul and Diaz-Leon (2018) indicate, is a recent feminist innovation. In sharing lived experiences, women were able to see a commonality to many of their problems, and thus originated the phrase sexual harassment. Naming the problem made tackling it simpler as well as raising people's consciousness about it.

By claiming that some terms encode a male worldview, Saul and Diaz-Leon suggest that the meanings of some words and terminologies appear to split up the world in ways that is normal for men (2018, online). Naming the feminist interests in language as the problem of male control over language, we are confronted with the theoretical issue of determining how language informs our worldview. Its answer can be theoretically traced to Sapir and Whorf's hypothesis that language determines worldview, and feminist researchers have based their work on this deterministic view, suggesting that the reason why the dominant worldview is androcentric is "because the conventions of language have been developed in a patriarchal context" (Cameron 1992, 30). If language, as Sapir and Whorf suggest, determines worldview, and language did develop in a patriarchal context, then it makes acceptable, to some extent, the arguments that feminists have put forward about language being male and how it has codified a male worldview.

In her groundbreaking work *Man Made Language*, Dale Spender adopts the Sapir–Whorfian deterministic hypothesis rather uncritically. Despite this, it served as a clarion call for raising feminists' consciousness about language. By asserting that language is a male invention, Spender does not mean that all words and rules of grammar have been devised or created by men; what she appears to mean is that linguistic terms have been defined from a male perspective excluding the views of their female counterparts. Even supposedly feminine terms like motherhood, which is situated in female experience, have been defined positively from a male perspective. Using this word in relation to the complicated experiences, both positive and negative, that women feel and undergo as mothers becomes awkward. In the words of Spender,

> Men may know something of motherhood – after all they comprise the majority of obstetricians – but they know only from their specific position as men, and only from the perspective of a spectator. This must provide a limited view of the event, for the meanings of motherhood which men have provided are based on the way in which motherhood relates to them. It would not be it all surprising if motherhood meant something entirely different to those who were the participants.
>
> (1990, 58)

Much as females might attempt to redefine motherhood, a conflict between experience and the language that describes the reality of women forces them into silence:

> for if "unhappy motherhood" is an oxymoron, might not the experience the woman is trying to express with it be equally bizarre? If she uses deviant language, will she herself be labelled unnatural and deviant, not fit to be a mother as men define the term? (Cameron 1992, 148)

Cameron advances Spender's view that the entire lexicon can be analysed in this way: "all words encode a male point of view" (1992, 149). While this may sound exaggerated, Cameron indicates that, "[W]here this point of view may be at odds with women's experience, women can either take it on anyway (alienation) or reject it (silence)" (1992). A last option which I add to the list is that women can also reform it.

Other aspects of language that feminist theorists have devoted attention to include gendered metaphors, speech act theory, the meaning of woman and the philosophy of language. Gendered metaphors are prejudiced comparisons which impose the experiences and orientations of one sex on the other. To unveil the impact of gendered metaphors on women, the feminist theorists Luce Irigaray and Genevieve Lloyd among others have utilized Jacques Derrida's analysis of the metaphorical origin of concepts. Lloyd contends that "the metaphor of maleness is deeply embedded in philosophical articulations of ideas and ideals of reason" (1993, viii). Phyllis Rooney (1991) similarly considers the impact of sex metaphors on conceptions of reason.

Two major departures from these concerns of feminist language reformers which are often listed under the substantial positive research programme as an improvement on the larger discipline of philosophy of language include the "use of the Speech act theory in feminist theorizing" as well as "on the meaning of woman." Jennifer Hornsby's (2000) and Rae Langton's (1993) works among others have been pivotal to this discourse and the discourse in turn has helped feminist philosophy of language gain mainstream popularity.

Hornsby (2000), in her work, attempts to foster a particular kind of speech act theory which she calls communicative speech acts. She proposes that this theory, if incorporated into 'malestream' philosophy of language, would amount to a feminist advancement of the discipline as well as become a repair of this masculine thought system. Langton, following Austin, extricates the three aspects of speech acts, submitting that pornography encourages rape through perlocutionary and illocutionary acts which then silence women. The duo of Hornsby and Langton (1998) pursue this line of thought in illuminating Catherine MacKinnon's assertion that pornography silences and subordinate women. Nancy Bauer (2015) and Lorna Finlayson (2014) have both raised critical objections to this view. In their opinion, feminist literature which claim that speech acts and pornography silence women are deeply misguided.

One important objective of this study has been to critically examine the concept of woman, by examining 'woman,' our endeavour has simply been to respond to the interrogation: What is the meaning of woman? Questions bothering on meaning are foundational to the field of philosophy of language, as such, the meaning of woman is a necessary introductory discourse for feminist philosophy of language in whatever cultural context. Haslanger's (2004) work, previously explored in Chapter 1, purposes to offer not only an explanation of the nature of gender, but also an explanation of the meaning of 'woman.' We explored its equivalent within the Yorùbá culture in Chapter 3.

These feminist concerns as detailed in our explorations above have witnessed significant reform efforts albeit with their own limitations. One reform effort which has witnessed little, or no limitation is the practice of employing the plural pronoun 'they' as a singular pronoun that is gender neutral. This has been because of feminist criticism on the assumed gender neutral 'he.' Bolaños Cuéllar Sergio observes the progressive instance of gender-marked language use as feminist language reform theorists have feminized the generic 'he' by replacing it with "pronouns (and nouns) in their feminine forms with a generic all inclusive meaning" (2006, 158). Another success story in the reform effort attempt by feminist philosophers of language is in making women more visible by seeking acceptable alternatives to the use of gender-specific occupational terms, as such, gender neutral occupational terms are more in use and gradually becoming more accepted. Aside from modifying language use, feminist language reform efforts have also seen to the creation of neologisms like, in addition to sexual harassment, "battered women," "Ms," "date rape" and "herstory" to both raise awareness of sexism and bring women and women's issues into the language" (Crawford & Fox 2007, 482). These reform attempts have in no way reached their limits as gendered power dynamics in language are still being shifted.

An African Feminist Philosophy of Language in Dialogue with the Feminist Philosophy of Language

Instituting a discipline intended to be an AFPL will more than likely shadow certain traditions from the feminist philosophy of language, African philosophy of language and the broader discipline of the philosophy of language. An AFPL, being an offshoot of these subdivisions, must interconnect and yet distinguish itself from its other counterparts.

A feminist philosophy of language as a reaction to malestream philosophy of language distinguishes itself from this body of work not by avoiding the interests of philosophy of language in meaning, reference and truth but by arguing that "these central topics in mainstream analytic philosophy of language cannot be properly investigated without attention to the social context in which language operates" (Wyatt n.d, online). Similarly, an AFPL as an attempt to reform male-controlled language through which the subjugation of the African woman occurs is a reaction to feminist philosophy of language as it obtains in the West. Instituting an AFPL, I opine, commenced by the deconstruction and reconstruction of sexist and oppressive proverbial language through the medium I forenamed feminist postproverbials. Like feminist philosophy of language, AFPL has enriched the mainstream philosophy of language by situating the oral tradition of proverbs, following Grice, as a form of implicature, as an instance of performatives and subsequently as an illustration of speech acts in communicative situations.

An AFPL differs from an African philosophy of language because it is not preoccupied with what has been called the language question in Africa – the question of what language we ought to do philosophy in. Rather than see language as a problem in Africa, AFPL perceives this heterogeneity an advantage to the discourse on woman and an enrichment to feminist theorising in Africa. The 'language problem' in Africa creates for feminist scholarship a robust and viable research field and is in fact a problem that opens the door to many continuities. Imagine an analysis on the meaning of woman in as many as 3000 languages and sexist proverbial disruptions in just as many!

Both are, however, equally invested in the collective fight against Eurocentrism and imperialism borne out of the reality of Africa's colonial experience. Like African philosophy of language, AFPL constitutes a radical attempt towards accomplishing the decolonization mission. Even though both have similar and dissimilar subject matters, they recognize that language plays a significant role in the decolonizing agenda for the continent. For instance, both coalesce around Wiredu's clarion call for conceptual decolonization as an irreducible agenda that speak to Africa's postcolonial predicament in all its ramifications.

Thus, as part of the conceptual decolonization task, the AFPL is faced with the initial conceptual objective of unravelling both the meaning and ideological boundaries of "woman." In rethinking woman, AFPL, like mainstream philosophy of language, will be occupied with *meaning:* "Questions about *meaning* belong in any philosophy of language. And when the topic is *meaning*, one might expect to find connections between malestream and feminists' agenda" (Hornsby 2000, 88).

Understanding the *meaning* of woman in specific cultural contexts open new concerns that could not find adequate answers anywhere else. The social context in which language is used is arguably a significant marker differentiating the preoccupations of the philosophy of language and the feminist philosophy of language. Similarly, the sociocultural context in which language is used is the 'differentiating factor' between the feminist philosophy of language and its African counterpart. Thus, to continue investigating concepts outside of the African sociocultural context would be unsuitable for Africa's existential situation. In the sociocultural terrain of Africa, the feminists' concern over language use changes almost entirely and this makes it an indigenous problem requiring an indigenous solution.

Feminist philosophy of language in the Western and African traditions is marked by remarkable differences. While false gender neutrality is a major concern among English speaking feminist language reformers, it loses potency on African soil. In *Language in Africa*, Edgar Gregersen notes that "Gender systems need not be based on categories that correspond to the European sex-linked ones. . . . In point of fact, sex-gender systems are relatively rare in Africa apart from Afro-Asiatic languages, which normally have masculine and feminine, but no neuter" (1977, 52). To be a bit more specific, Yorùbá language has no gender specific word, like 'man' in the English language, which is supposedly used as a gender-neutral word to denote humans. The Yorùbá term *Okunrin* denotes the social category man, and *Obinrin*, woman. While "man" poses as gender neutral in the English language, denoting a class of humans or humanity, *eniyan* is the Yorùbá word for humans and humanity.

The analysis of gendered pronouns is equally analogous. Whereas "he" and "she" feature as the pronouns for male and female respectively in English language, Musa Dube observes that "[T]urning to West Africa some languages do not have gendered pronouns. The names of God/Diety, therefore, appears as primarily gender neutral" (2012, 134). Although my major preoccupation is not on religion, it is important to note that whereas most African languages do not ascribe a gender to a Supreme *Being*, the English term "God/deity" is expressed as significantly male.

Expanding more on pronouns, P.J.L. Frankl posits that,

> In many Indo-European and Semitic languages, the pronoun is a major linguistic expression of gender; for example, the English third person singular pronoun is distinguished according to gender, although first and second person and the third person plural are not. . . . Despite recent efforts within the English-speaking world to promote language which does not manifest overt grammatical contrasts between masculine and feminine gender, the

inherent sexism of the generic masculine remains. By contrast, Swahili has a sex-neutral third person singular pronoun in the word *yeye* (which may mean either "he" or "she").

(1993, 86–87)

Oyeronke Oyewumi equally argues that in the Yorùbá language,

> all pronouns are ungendered. The third-person pronouns *ó* and *wón* make a distinction between older and younger in social interactions. Thus the pronoun *wón* is used to refer to an older person, irrespective of anatomic sex. Like the old English "thou" or the French pronoun *vous*, *wón* is the pronoun of respect and formality. *Ó* is used in situations of familiarity and intimacy.

(2005, 107)

With respect to the Igbo language of Nigeria, Ifi Amadiume corroborates this view:

> in subject pronouns, no distinction is made between male and female. The third person singular, *O*, stands for both male and female, unlike the English gender construction, which distinguishes male and female as "he" and "she." ... The genderless word *mmadu*, humankind, applies to both sexes. There is no usage as there is in English, of the word 'man' to represent both sexes.

(1987, 89)

Regarding gender-specific occupation terms, we hit both a parallel and a distinction. Both the Western and African traditions, with specific reference to the English and Yorùbá languages, have gender specific terms describing the work humans do. Among the Yorùbá, lineages have specialized occupations that distinguishes them and often reflects in the *oriki* (lineage praise chant) of the family. These occupations are usually gendered. Males follow in their lineage's specialized industries like blacksmithing, hunting and drumming while women tend to pick up skills like pottery, mat weaving, hair dressing and food preservation. While occupations are gendered, merchandise trading and general commerce are often performed by all. Thus, *alata* (pepper salesperson), *alaso* (clothes merchant), *oniresi* (rice merchant), *eleran* (butcher), *eleedu* (charcoal merchant) and so on, describes the nature of the trade being performed or goods being sold without necessarily revealing the biological sex of the person engaging in the trade. Sometimes, the prefix *Iya* (mother or female person), *Baba* (father or male person) or *omo* (child, either male or female) may be added as a way of addressing the person, this should not be seen as a way of gendering the occupation. It should be noted that modernity has made even lineage occupations which were hitherto gendered accessible to both sexes apart from few sacred ones like hunting, which is still a predominantly male-only occupation.

African Feminist Philosophy of Language: Current Trends, Future Prospects

Much as there have been various feminist language reform efforts involving the invention of new terms (like sexual harassment) or the use of alternative terms (like "they" instead of the generic "he"), there have also been attempts at reforming language that disparage woman within the academia in Africa. These different efforts, especially if they follow the feminist agenda and can be mined for philosophical readings, count essentially as works in AFPL. An African feminist philosophy of language, as earlier explicated, is an attempt to build on the indigenous. It is characterized by attention to not just the social context of language use but even more specifically to the cultural context with the objective of detecting and altering sexist connotations and patriarchal language and terminologies through different forms of linguistic disruptions. A good example of this is the feminist postproverbial method I adopted in this work in altering a significant part of sexist proverbial language. An important point to note about the relationship between feminist postproverbials as a method for linguistic disruptions and AFPL is that the discipline stands as a critique of the method. Philosophy, as a mode of and framework for thinking, plays a fundamental role in spurring people to think and criticise the ideas encompassing what they do (Afolayan 2024, 24). Since criticism permits philosophy to question established ideas and methods, AFPL's criticism of its own methods stands to open a discursive space for the creation of new theories and concepts.

Helen Yitah's "proverbial revolt" a similar method to the feminist postproverbials seeks to undermine the same proverbial aspect of our oral traditions, but we see a different kind of language reform in the work of Wanjira Muthoni, a Kenyan feminist and purveyor of the gender sensitization programme called the literary road to empowerment. Muthoni builds on the indigenous with the objective of sensitizing novelists, playwrights and booklovers on gender biases and encouraging innovative story telling by reconstructing old narratives and by telling new stories in the pattern of old narratives. Muthoni's argument is that the existing oral narratives are shaped by the patriarchal values which have moulded the society and so the mindset that the males must be in control is factored into these oral narratives thus encouraging the entrenchment of unequal gender relations (Arndt 2000, 713). In this vein, the oral literature mirrors and reproduces existing gender relations. Muthoni satisfies the feminist agenda by identifying and retelling these narratives in a new form as a strategic approach to not only sensitize the society, but to persuasively change the image and perception of women. In an interview with Susan Arndt, Muthoni reveals that while it might be impossible to change adults, the aim is to target children and hope to change how they perceive themselves as well as others. Doing this she opines is tantamount to changing adults, thus a whole generation would have been impacted (2000, 715).

Muthoni's literary reformative attempt, although laudable, has however faced a few challenges. As Yitah notes, the hostile response to Muthoni's (re)formed folktales steers us to safely conclude that the success of any effort to modify traditional oral literature is dependent upon a progressive enforcement of the change within its oral culture (2006, 238). This is simply because attempting to enforce oral reformations through written accounts especially on a society that is largely oral, as Muthoni did, was a summons for hostility and antagonism from a public who identified their culture to its oral narratives (ibid).[2] Since the success of any rhetorical act or situation depends largely on the audience we suggest that for a successful reformative attempt, alternative rhetorical attempts within AFPL must seek to work predominantly within the genre it emanated from. Sexist language must be identified within the various oral traditions, reformed in the academy and circulated into the larger society as *doxa* but still largely retain its oral form as a part of the tradition it emerged from. This means, for example, that, reconstructed proverbs which follow the feminist postproverbial method must still retain its form as a proverb and must be used in the same way as traditional proverbs. Similarly, oral literature, which Muthoni retells, must be orally transmitted. Thus, the mass media of radio, TV and movies and the new media of blogs, comedy skits, short musical clips, alongside traditional/informal forms of communication like moonlight storytelling, must be employed to ensure the success of these language reforms.

Other forms of linguistic disruptions exist unknown to us or unavailable to us at the time of this research. Being a work in its developing stages, discerning all possible prospects of an AFPL might be arduous. However, so long as it occurs as a form of language and it is demeaning to woman, especially those which can be identified as a part of the African oral tradition, it is worth disrupting, altering and reforming. We will briefly consider the rhetorical space of tweets. In the introductory section of this work, we signalled everyday sexism as another significant aspect that an AFPL need investigate. Cataloguing tweets from elitist subjects, Simidele Dosekun notes that "patriarchal power does not simply retreat as women advance" (2023, 1442). Despite the desirable qualities of rationality, strength, wealth, inventiveness and independence which define the elite modern Nigerian woman, her empowerment has yet to inhibit the brute force of patriarchy. These seemingly strong and independent women are maligned and belittled in public spaces with the aim of silencing them and "putting them in their place," beneath men.[3] Let us consider this tweet from Dosekun's collection:

> "#BeingfemaleinNigeria Him: How dare you talk back! I have your kind at home washin my clothes! Useless Akowe woman. Just because I hit ur car."
> (2023, 1440)

According to Dosekun, this tweet is written in the voice of a man who despite being at fault in a car accident with a woman driver "dismisses the woman's protestations, indeed her very right to protest, by reminding her that ultimately, she is not a subject to him but an object: a woman, of which he 'possesses' one himself, back at home doing his chores" (ibid). While these tweets were welcomed with fervour and experienced exponential growth in publicity – so much so that a reprisal hashtag on what it is to be male in Nigeria accompanied it – such everyday sexist stories need to go beyond cataloguing and analyzing to using the same rhetorical spaces to subvert such social control speech forms, turning vocabulary against those who had once used it as a weapon (Crick 2014, 253).

Another viable prospect would be to engage critically with concepts such as motherhood in African languages and its supposed association with suffering. For example, among the Yorùbá, *ìyá* (the term for motherhood) is poetically linked with *ìyà*[4] (the term for sorrow, misery and burden). This seems to suggest that sorrow and misery are regular features of motherhood. In another vein, the Yorùbá term for orgasm, *dà*, appears to encode a male worldview describing an act synonymous with "pouring," which would describe orgasm from a male perspective as ejaculation. It will interest this body of work to establish through research the universality of this occurrence in other African languages. These would help give credence to the idea that perhaps some African languages are supposedly borne out of some male perspective.

An African feminist philosophy of language will benefit tremendously from the creation and inclusion of various stimulating feminist fiction and non-fiction series, especially if they interrogate our worldview as Africans and seek to alter the status quo of the reigning patriarchal order. Many of these fiction works abound, and their authors are celebrated as African women writers. It is worth noting that women writing in a male-dominated context is itself a subversive act! Buchi Emecheta, Chimamanda Adichie and Mariama Ba, to mention a few, have successfully moved women from the sidelines to the core in the literary field and have as well shifted women from supporting roles to lead roles in their novels. The aim, however, is to go beyond bringing woman to the fore to changing the rhetoric for woman through their novels. Emerging feminist authors and bloggers also have important roles to play in entrenching a new rhetorical tradition. Employing parodies in prose with a constructive intent rather than a negative one can aid the reimagining and rewriting of aspects of texts considered sexist or misogynistic.[5] Parodies can also aid a "renarration" of aspects of canonical feminist texts which thematically and stylistically bore resemblance to the androcentric language of its time. Similarly, songs composed with the aim to disrupt and reform the linguistic space for woman while empowering and emancipating the African woman should suffice as part of works that can be categorized under this new rhetorical tradition. Indeed, every aspect of popular culture that is dehumanizing for woman should experience such feminist reformations.

Towards an African Feminist Philosophy of Language 111

Efforts such as are required to thoroughly ground an AFPL would require a multidisciplinary and interdisciplinary approach to succeed. Significantly, this exposition has had to glean insights from a variety of disciplines. Thus, AFPL must be substantiated in feminist perspectives from literary studies, history, sociology, religious studies, education, linguistics, African language studies, cultural studies and other disciplines. Much like how the larger body of African feminisms enjoys a multidisciplinary approach, this linguistic turn in African feminism will thrive both on multidisciplinary and interdisciplinary approaches.

Notes

1 See, for example, this teaser: https://riddlesbrainteasers.com/old-gray-surgeon/
2 Balogun (2010) also makes this noteworthy observation in my erstwhile discussion.
3 I similarly argued in Chapter 3 how historically, women who performed heroic feats were disparaged by men.
4 Note the tonal difference between the two terms.
5 Kiru Taye's "Thighs Fell Apart" is a good example of a parodied prose. For analysis, see Yeku, J. (2017). Thighs Fell Apart. *Journal of African Cultural Studies*, Vol. 29, No. 3, pp. 261–275.

References

Afolayan, A. 2024. Proverbs, Postproverbials and the African Mythological Imaginary. In Postproverbials at Work: The Context of Radical Proverb-Making in Nigerian Languages. Ed. Aderemi Raji-Oyelade. *Proverbium*, Online Supplement 4.

Amadiume, I. 1987. *Male Daughters, Female Husbands: Gender and Sex in an African Society.* London, UK: Zed Books.

Arndt, S. 2000. African Gender Trouble and African Womanism: An Interview with Chikwenye Ogunyemi and Wanjira Muthoni. *Signs*, 25(3). The University of Chicago Press.

Balogun, O.A. 2010. Proverbial Oppression of Women in Yoruba African Culture: A Philosophical Overview. *Thought and Practice: A Journal of the Philosophical Association of Kenya* (PAK) New Series. Vol. 2. 1.

Bauer, N. 2015. *How to Do Things with Pornography.* Cambridge: Harvard University Press.

Bodine, A. 1998. Androcentrism in Prescriptive Grammar: Singular 'They,' Sex-Indefinite 'He,' and 'He or She.' In *Feminist Critique of Language: A Reader.* Ed. D. Cameron. London & New York: Routledge, 124–138.

Bolaños Cuéllar, S. 2006. Women's Language: A Struggle to Overcome Inequality. *Forma y Función.* 158. Accessed online 29 December 2020. https://www.researchgate.net/publication/238766777_Women%27s_language_a_struggle_to_overcome_inequality

Cameron, D. 1992. *Feminism and Linguistic Theory.* Basingstoke and London: Macmillan Press Ltd.

Crawford, M. & Fox, A. 2007. IX From Sex to Gender and Back Again: Co-optation of a Feminist Language Reform. *Feminism & Psychology*, 17(4). Sage.
Crick, N. 2014. Rhetoric and Events. *Philosophy & Rhetoric*, 47(3). University Park, PA: Penn State University Press.
Dosekun, S. 2023. The problems and intersectional politics of "#BeingFemaleinNigeria". *Feminist Media Studies*, 23(4): 1429–1445. https://doi.org/10.1080/14680777.2022.2030386
Dube, M.W. 2012. Postcolonial Feminist Perspectives on African Religions. In *The Wiley-Blackwell Companion to African Religions*. Ed. E.K. Bongmba. Oxford, UK: Wiley-Blackwell.
DuBois, E.C. et al. 1987. *Feminist Scholarship: Kindling in the Groves of Academe*. Urbana & Chicago: University of Illinois Press.
Ehrlich, S. & King, R. 1998. Gender-Based Language Reform and the Social Construction of Meaning. In *Feminist Critique of Language: A Reader*. Ed. D. Cameron. London & New York: Routledge.
Finlayson, L. 2014. How to Screw Things with Words. *Hypatia*, 29(4).
Frankl, P.J.L. 1993. The Indifference to Gender in Swahili and other Bantu Languages. *South African Journal of African Languages*, 13(3).
Gregersen, E.A. 1977. *Language in Africa: An Introductory Survey*. New York, Paris & London: Gordon and Breach.
Haslanger, S. 2004. Future Genders? Future Races? *Philosophic Exchange* 34 (1): 1–24. http://digitalcommons.brockport.edu/phil_ex/vol34/iss1/1
Hornsby, J. & 1998. Free Speech and Illocution. *Legal Theory*, 4(1). pp 21–37. doi:10.1017/S1352325200000902.
Hornsby, J. 2000. "Feminism in Philosophy of Language: Communicative Speech Acts", in The Cambridge Companion to Feminism in Philosophy. Eds. Miranda Fricker and Jennifer Hornsby. 87–106. doi:10.1017/CCOL0521624517.006. *Feminism in Philosophy*. Cambridge: Cambridge University Press.
Langton, R. 1993. Speech Acts and Unspeakable Acts. *Philosophy and Public Affairs*, 22(4): 293–330. Reprinted with minor changes in Langton 2009d, 25–64.
Lloyd, G. 1993. *The Man of Reason: "Male" and "Female" in Western Philosophy*. Second edition. London, UK: Routledge.
Mercier, A. 1995. A Perverse Case of the Contingent A Priori: On the Logic of Emasculating Language (A Reply to Dawkins and Dummett). *Philosophical Topics*, 23(2): 221–259.
Moulton, J. 1981. The Myth of the Neutral 'Man'. In: Vetterling-Braggin, M., Ed., Sexist Language, Littlefield and Adams, Paterson, 100–115.
Oyewumi, O. 2005. (Re)Constituting the Cosmology and Sociocultural Institutions of Oyó-Yorùbá. In *African Gender Studies: A Reader*. Ed. O. Oyewumi. New York: Palgrave Macmillan.
Penelope, J. 1990. *Speaking Freely: Unlearning the Lies of the Fathers' Tongues*. New York, NY: Pergamon.
Rooney, P. 1991. Gendered Reason: Sex Metaphor and Conceptions of Reason. *Hypatia*, 6(2).

Saul, J. & Diaz-Leon, E. 2018. Feminist Philosophy of Language. In *Stanford Encyclopedia of Philosophy.* Ed. Edward N. Zalta. https://plato.stanford. edu/archives/fall2018/entries/feminism-language/
Spender, D. 1990. *Man Made Language.* Second edition. London, UK: Pandora.
Wyatt, N. n.d. https://philpapers.org/browse/feminist-philosophy-of-language. Accessed online 30 December 2020.
Yitah, H. 2006. Throwing Stones in Jest: Kasena Women's "Proverbial" Revolt. *Oral Tradition.* 21(2).

Index

acclivity theorists 11
Achonulu, Catherine 12
Adegbindin, Omotade 67
Adichie, Chimamanda 110
Afolayan, Adeshina ix–x, 33, 37, 57, 79, 108
Africana Womanism 12
African feminism 2, 4, 12, 43, 81, 83, 111
African feminist philosophy of language AFPL viii–ix, 1–5, 34, 36, 40, 66, 81–82, 97, 105–111
African philosophy of language 34.36, 105
agrarian 43, 45–47, 49, 52, 61
agriculture 45–46, 49
Akan 49–51, 54, 61
Aniwura, Efunsetan 64–66, 68, 94
anti-proverbs 77–78
ara 54, 88, 91
aya 14, 88

Ba, Mariama 2, 110
Balogun, Oladele Abiodun 84–86, 91
Bantu 49–50, 59, 62
Black feminism 10
bride service 49, 51

Christianity 52
class 4, 9–12, 14–16, 20–22, 24, 35, 40, 56, 82, 106
complementarity 12–13, 55
Crick, Nathan 3, 35, 110

de Beauvoir, S 16–17, 20, 57
declension theorists 11
decolonisation 2, 5, 28–34, 37–38, 40, 43, 53, 82, 105
decolonised feminisms 8
Diop, Cheikh Anta 48–49, 51–52
Dosekun, Simidele 3, 109–110
doxa 39–40, 85, 109

ecological 20, 23; thinking 23
Emecheta, Buchi 2, 110
èmí 54
Engels, Friedrich 46–47, 52, 60
episteme 39–40, 85
epistemicide 31
essentialism 16, 18, 44, 53
essentialist 16–18, 48
everyday sexism 3, 109

Fanon, F 28–30
Farrar, Tarikhu 49–51
feminist philosophy of language 104–106
feminist theory 4, 8–9, 12, 15–17, 22
Friedan, Betty 9–10
functionalist 44

gender 2–5, 8, 11–21, 24–25, 35–36, 43–44, 48, 53, 55–58, 61–66, 81–84, 100–104, 106–108
gender relative morality 56
Grant, Judith 8, 23
Grice, H. P. 75, 105

Haslanger, Sally 18−20, 53, 104
hooks, bell 9−11, 22
hunter/gatherer 45−47, 49, 62

Ijala 66−68
imperialism 28, 33, 37, 53, 105;
 cultural 13, 21−23; linguistic 33
implicature 75−76, 105
industrialisation 47−48, 93
intersectional, intersectionality 3,
 11−12, 15, 82
Ipadeola, Abosede 4, 39, 56
irua 58
Islam 52
Ìyá 57, 59, 61−63, 65, 107, 110
Ìyà (suffering) 59, 61
Ìyà mi, Àjé (cult) 62

language games 77
Lawuyi, Olatunde 55
life form 77
linguistic community 76−77
Litovkina, Anna 77−78

maigira 50
marginalisation 4, 21
Marxist 22, 60
matriarchy 5, 43, 48−51, 63
matrilineal 46−47, 49−50, 52
menstruation 58−59, 61
metaphors 24, 81, 103
metaphysics 12, 34, 50, 53−56
Mieder, Wolfgang 73, 76−78
Mignolo, W 5, 28−29, 31−32, 39
misogynist 2−3, 5, 86, 91, 110
Moremi 64−65, 94
motherism 12
movement, feminist 10−14, 17, 20,
 24, 29
Muthoni, Wanjira 2, 108−109
mythistories 63

Nkealah, Naomi 12
Nzegwu, Nkiru 4

Obìnrin 57−59, 61, 63, 67, 89−92, 106
odu Òseètúrá 62−63

Ogundipe-Leslie, Molara 11, 13
Ogunleye, Foluke 66
Ogunyemi, Chikwenye 12−13
ohemmaa 49−50
Oko 15, 89−90
Olajubu, Oyeronke 57−59
Omolúàbí 54−55
oppression viii−ix, 4−6, 10−13, 15,
 18, 20−25, 30, 43−44, 47, 67,
 72, 81, 84, 86, 88
orí-inú 54
oriki 64, 107
Osha, Sanya 4−5
Osun 62−65, 94
Owomoyela, Oyekan 72, 76,
 87, 92
Oyeleye, Olayinka viii−ix, 56, 79
Oyewumi, Oyeronke 2, 11, 14, 57,
 61−63, 107
Oyowe, Oritsegbubemi 54−56

Pabir 50−51, 62
paremiology viii−ix, 81−82
parody 2, 80
patriarchy 5, 13, 25, 43−44, 47−49,
 51−53, 55, 62, 67, 82−83, 85,
 96, 109
patrilineal 47, 50
personhood 43, 53−56, 58,
 61−63
philosophy of language 34−36.74,
 77, 100, 103−106
plough 9, 45, 48
popular culture 1−2, 34, 85−86, 110
postmodern ix, 2−3, 79−80, 82, 86
postproverbial 2, 6, 40, 72, 77, 82,
 84, 86; feminist 2, 40, 77, 81−82,
 85−86, 105, 108
poststructural 2−3, 79−82
pragmatics 74
prehistory 43, 45
production, knowledge 3, 5, 23, 28,
 30, 37−38, 82
production/reproduction 38, 46−48,
 52, 60−61, 93
proverbs viii, 2, 5−6, 35−36, 40,
 67−68, 72−97, 105, 109

queenmother 49–51, 61

race 4, 11–12, 19–20, 24, 35–36, 40, 82
rhetoric 3–4, 13, 36, 64, 74, 85, 87, 110
rite, of passage 55, 58–59

Said, E. 29
Schipper, Mineke 87, 89, 96–97
Sereres 52
sexism 3, 8, 10–11, 22–23, 65, 104, 107, 109
Spender, Dale 100, 102–103
Spivak, G. 28–30, 38, 82
subaltern 29–30
suffrage rights 8, 15

Thiong 'O, Ngugi wa 23, 28, 36–37
Truth, Sojourner 9–10, 16

violence 21–23, 29–30, 32, 35; domestic 87; epistemic 2, 30, 82

Walker, Alice 12
Washington, Teresa 62
Wingo, Ajume 54
Wittgenstein, Ludwig 34, 74, 77, 79–80
Witts, Charlotte 53
woman 1–6
womanism 12

Yitah, Helen 2, 85–87, 92, 109
Yoruba 5, 40–41, 43, 53–55, 57–66, 72, 76, 78, 83–84, 87–88, 90–95, 104, 106–107, 110

Zeleza, Tiyambe 48

For Product Safety Concerns and Information please contact our EU representative GPSR@taylorandfrancis.com
Taylor & Francis Verlag GmbH, Kaufingerstraße 24, 80331 München, Germany

www.ingramcontent.com/pod-product-compliance
Lightning Source LLC
Chambersburg PA
CBHW071822230426
43670CB00013B/2544